Ideas for fabric printing and dyeing

Peter H Gooch

Ideas for fabric printing and dyeing

Charles Scribner's Sons · New York

First published in Great Britain by B T Batsford Ltd
Printed in Great Britain
Library of Congress Catalog Card Number 74–4816
ISBN 0 684 14066 7

Contents

Acknowledgment

Foreword

The author wishes to thank Mr and Mrs J Murphy for their helpful advice; Mrs L R Davies for information on needlework; Mrs K Jameson for advice on batik; Mr D Hawkins and the Commercial Photographic Service of Streatham for their help with the photographs; and his wife for her patience in typing the manuscript.

London 1974   PG

This book is intended for beginners or near beginners in fabric design, and emphasizes the simpler and less expensive aspects of the craft. Recent advances by manufacturers in the development of dyes and other materials have made it much more simple to carry out the various techniques than formerly. However, for those who wish to go more deeply into the subject and who feel that they require more detailed information, a bibliography of fabric design and allied crafts is given at the end of this book.

Each section of this book is devoted to a different aspect of fabric design and is introduced with a brief description of the craft, followed by as many ideas as possible, each being prefixed with a list of the materials required, and in most cases accompanied by at least one illustration of the idea.

It is not intended that the book should necessarily be followed as arranged, and of course the techniques can be used singly or in any combination desired.

The ideas are not intended to be copied but should be seen as starting points for further experiment and exploration.

Introduction

The working area for fabric printing should be as spacious and clean as possible. A sink with cold water is essential and preferably hot water as well.

For block and screen printing the table should be wide enough to take fabrics of the maximum width desired, and also long enough to accommodate a useful length of material. If it is not possible to have a long table, the fabric may be rolled round a roller, such as a broom handle or cardboard tube, at one end, while the other end is being printed. However, it is preferable not to move the fabric during the printing operation. If it has to be moved each section should be completed in all colours before moving the cloth, otherwise it will be found difficult to obtain a correct registration. The table should be heavy and stable, and the top flat and firm. Cover the top of the table with a single piece of carpet underfelt or blanket. Stretch this tight and tack it all the way round beneath the edge of the table. Stretch a sheet of water-proof material over this and tack it in the same way.

An undercloth should be put down on the table below the fabric that is to be printed. This will absorb excess dye which penetrates the printed material, and will help to keep the waterproof cloth clean. It can be washed from time to time. This undercloth should be of a fairly absorbent material, but need not be expensive. Unbleached Indian cotton is suitable for this. It may be stuck down with a gum or resin preparation; formulae and manufacturers of these are given at the end of the book. This adhesive is poured along one end of the table and spread over it in a thin film with a squeegee. The undercloth is then unrolled from one end and spread smoothly over the table with a warm iron so that it sticks to the gummed surface.

The printer should know the nature of the fibres in the cloth he proposes to use. In general a better result is obtained when using a natural fibre rather than an artificial one: if in doubt, it should be possible to discover the nature of the fibre from the shop or manufacturer where the cloth is obtained. The cloth must be thoroughly washed before use to remove any chemicals which may have been put in by the manufacturer. This will help the fabric to take the dye more readily. Soaking in water overnight before washing will help. Old sheets and other linen which have been washed a great deal will not require this initial scouring, and are good for experimental work.

The material on which the design is to be made must be absolutely smooth when ironed out on the table-top. Pin it along all its edges to the backcloth. This prevents any movement during the printing operation. When screen-printing cover these pins with adhesive tape to prevent their damaging the gauze of the screen.

The dyes or printing inks to be used will depend on the nature of the printing process; these will be dealt with under the appropriate sections.

There are various pieces of equipment which are essential to success in this work: a rubber hose or shower spray to attach to the taps of the sink is useful for washing down screens and sink. Plenty of newspaper should always be available. Other useful items are

Pencils
erasers
cartridge paper
drawing boards
rulers
drawing pins
(thumbtacks)
tracing paper
inks
poster or gouache
paints
various sizes of
paintbrushes, both
hair and bristle,
scissors
newsprint or kitchen-
paper

adhesive tape
brown gumstrip paper
pins
small plastic bowls
or jars with
airtight lids
large plastic bowls
for dyeing
rubber gloves
spoons
thread
string
elastic bands
strong waterproof
adhesive and an
iron, preferably a
steam iron.

Stamp or block printing

This section deals with printing from a surface which has been charged with dye or ink and then pressed onto fabric to leave an impression. The surface can be anything from traditional materials, such as wood or lino, to sections of vegetables, or materials such as card, corrugated glass or cork, or even thumb prints.

Some printing can be done direct from the object, such as potato prints or the edge of a piece of card or end of a stick. With other materials, it is more convenient to attach them to a block through which the pressure is transmitted and which can be held firmly and comfortably in the hand. This block should be of bonded wood and should be at least 12 mm ($\frac{1}{2}$ in.) thick. Its other dimensions will depend on the size of the motif required. Prints can be made from small blocks by hand pressure. With larger blocks it is usual to strike the back of the block with the handle of a mallet, the head of the mallet providing the necessary weight. Wood blocks must not warp, and it is a good idea to varnish them to make them completely waterproof. Blocks may be made by cutting away parts of the surface leaving other areas raised, or by building up materials on the

surface. Whatever is attached to the block to make the printing surface should be fixed with a strong waterproof adhesive.

Colours for fabric printing may be oil or water based. The oil based inks are easy to apply but tend to spoil the 'feel' of the fabric because of the layer of ink which lies on the surface of the material. Water based dyes penetrate and do not spoil the quality of the cloth. They are also translucent and therefore tend to give brighter colours and can be overprinted. Difficulty may be found in getting the dye to cover the surface of the block well. This tends to make the printed impression slightly mottled which can be an attractive element in the design, but on the other hand may not be desired. To overcome this, the surface of the block can be roughened with glass paper to make it hold the dye more evenly. Place the block face downwards onto a medium rough sheet of glasspaper and rub with a circular motion to score the surface.

Alternatively, the block can be flocked. Flocking is a wool or rayon powder which, when applied to the surface of the block, makes it more absorbent. Put a small amount of mordant, which is a sticky ink, onto a sheet of glass or other non-absorbent surface. Roll the ink out evenly, then transfer it to the face of the block with the roller until all the raised parts are well covered. Sprinkle flocking powder over the tacky areas till the block is covered. Put a board on top and press the powder down, then leave it to dry for 24 hours. After this the surface powder can be shaken off, collected and used again.

Designs for block printing on fabric should be bold and open, as the printing dye tends to fill in any fine details. Water based dyes used for screen printing are also suitable for block printing, but need to be made up to a slightly thicker consistency. Add a thickening solution made up of water and *Manutex*. The formula for this is given at the end of the book. Mix this gum solution with the dye till the right degree of tackiness required is reached. Oil based inks may be applied by roller. Put the ink onto a glass plate or other non-absorbent surface. Roll it out evenly, then coat the face of the block by rolling the ink over it in all directions. Water based dyes need to be applied from a printing pad. An effective pad can be made from a fairly thick piece of carpet underfelt or sponge which should be slightly larger than the printing block. Glue this pad to a large tin lid, saucer, or to a piece of hardboard. Press the face of the block into the pad which has been charged with dye, turning it each time to distribute the colour evenly. For successful printing all the operations must be regular—charging and re-charging the pad, and pressing the block to the pad and to the

1   The printing table with the fabric prepared for printing (see page 28)

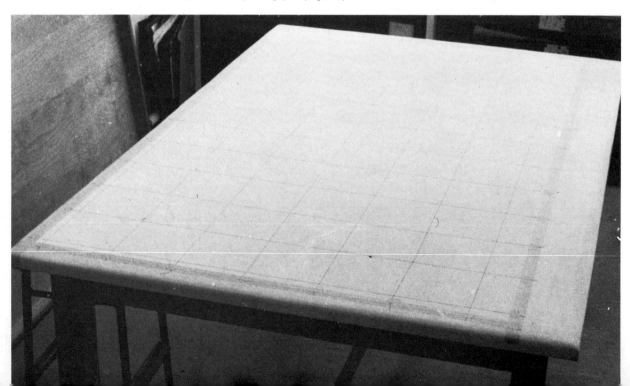

fabric with equal weight. The table and fabric should be prepared as described in the introduction. The cloth should not need to be marked out as for screen printing, as it is much easier to see where to place the block accurately.

A simple unit repeat

A good way to begin to explore the possibilities of pad or block printing is to take a simple unit and repeat it in as many different ways as possible. A fingerprint, for example, will make a very simple oval shape but apart from changing the colour, variety can be achieved

by overprinting, by the amount of pressure applied, by spacing and by the direction of lines. It will then be seen that it is not necessary to have a complex motif to produce an interesting design.
Figure 2

Roller prints

Printing pad or plate, turps substitute, roller (composition, rubber or sponge), newsprint, clean rag, printing ink or dye, palette knife

The roller itself can be used for printing direct onto the fabric. Small rollers are the most flexible to use. A variety of effects can be obtained by overlapping the shapes, varying

2   Fingerprint pattern on cloth

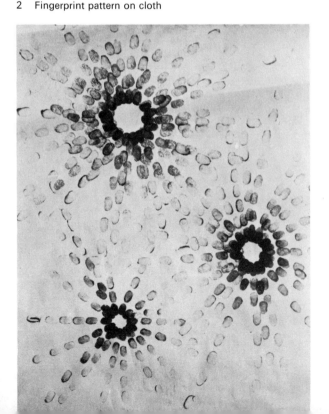

3   Roller print on fabric

the pressure and direction of the movement of the roller, as well as by changing the colour. The roller may be of hard rubber or gelatine composition, which are most suited to oil based inks, or sponge rubber, such as is used for painting walls and ceilings. These take pigment dye well and make good textured backgrounds to other forms of overprinting.

A pattern can be incised with a saw or chisel, or drilled into the surface of a wooden roller so that it will print as a continuous repeat. An old rolling pin is ideal for this purpose.
Figure 3

Printing with various materials
Wood block, waterproof glue, dye or printing ink, printing pad or inking plate, roller, turps substitute, clean rag, newspaper, newsprint

Provided the ink or dye can be made to adhere, any material can be used as a printing surface.

5   A print from a thick card cut and mounted on a wood block

6   Felt makes a good printing surface because it holds the dye pigment well

4   Design printed from the end of a matchbox and tip of a matchstick

7 A print made from pieces of felt cut to shape and mounted on a wood block

The design will naturally depend very much on the nature of the material used. Card, wood, plastic, felt, sponge, rubber, string, wire, leather, sacking, cork, plaster, clay, are a few of the materials which in various forms can be cut, arranged and glued to a block to make excellent prints.
Figures 4–9

8 Corrugated cardboard makes an effective printing surface. It should be glued to a piece of rigid material such as a wood-block

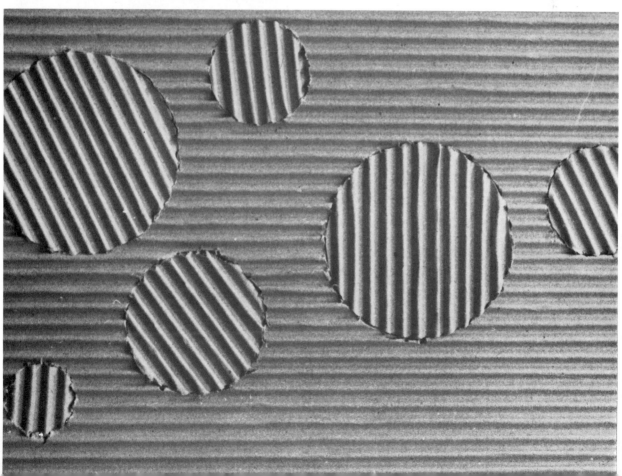

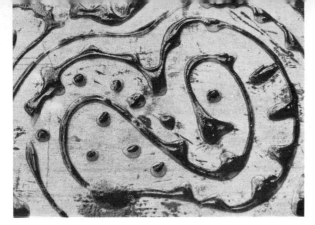

9 PVA dripped onto a woodblock makes an effective printing surface when dry

leaf satisfactorily, and it will be found that oil based fabric printing inks are more effective. The leaf can be glued to a block, but it is possible to print an unsupported leaf without damaging or smudging it. Roll out the ink onto a printing plate, which can consist of a sheet of glass or other non-absorbent surface. Put the tip of one finger on the end of the leaf and roll the ink on away from the finger. This will ensure that the leaf does not wrap itself around the roller. Place the leaf face down on the cloth, put a piece of thin paper over it, and press the leaf to the cloth with the fingers or with a clean roller.

The above procedure applies to other objects such as feathers, grasses, seaweed, pressed flowers, and lace.
Figure 10

Leaf prints

Leaves, fabric printing ink, printing plate, roller, newspaper, turps substitute, clean rag

Usually the veined side of the leaf, at the back, is the more interesting. Pigment dyes may be used, but it is difficult to get these to cover the

10 Leaf print on cotton fabric

Potato cuts

Potato, sharp knife, pigment dye, spoon, printing pad, newsprint paper, clean rag, iron

Cut the potato in half and press the cut surface into the printing pad. See how many interesting patterns can be made by combining the simple oval shape in various ways. Follow this by cutting the surface of the potato in a simple way. V-shaped cuts should be made with the blade of a sharp knife and the area between the cuts removed. This will ensure a strong printing surface. More complex motifs can be cut after experience has been gained,

11 Potato cut print using pigment dye on a background previously patterned with a batik design

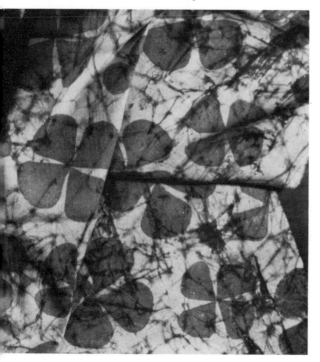

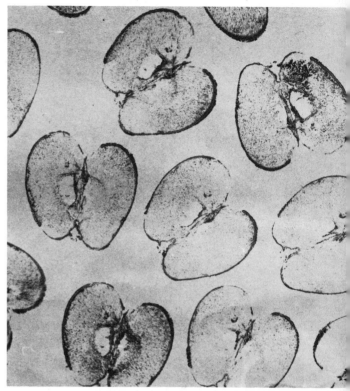

12 Fabric print of a half section of an apple

but it is not possible to cut very complicated shapes. More complex designs can be made by combining simple shapes when printing. Only a limited amount of printing can be done from one potato because of its fragile nature, and it is not possible to keep it because it will shrivel up. However, it should be possible to print a square yard or so of cloth. If the potato does start to disintegrate in the middle of a piece of work, the solution is to cut another design as like as possible to the first.
Figure 11

15

13 Polystyrene printing block. The top block was made by heating keys on a hotplate and placing them on the block so that they melted through, the lower block by dripping *Bostik* onto it

Polystyrene printing blocks

Polystyrene, knife or electric cutter for polystyrene, wood block, printing ink or dye, spoon, printing pad or inking plate, turps substitute, newsprint, newspaper, clean rag

Prints can be made from polystyrene blocks or sheets. If it is in sheet form, it is advisable to mount it on a wood block. It may be cut with a sharp knife or with a blade which has been heated in a flame or on a hotplate. Metal objects may be heated and placed on the polystyrene, and they will melt their way through, leaving a clear cut image in the material. There are many forms of polystyrene cutters on the market which are heated by electricity. These are cheap and effective, but it is not difficult to make similar devices. An electric soldering-iron is a useful tool for designing on polystyrene, also certain chemicals have a dissolving power on polystyrene, and can be painted or dribbled onto it to indent the surface.

Figure 13

16

Colour plate 1   Lino cut and string print. *Printex* pigment dyes on white cotton

Clay printing blocks

Clay, two sticks, rolling pin, knife, kiln, printing ink, printing plate, turps substitute, newsprint, newspaper, clean rag

Put the clay on the table between two sticks of about 305 mm (12 in.) × 19 mm $\frac{3}{4}$ in. × 12 mm ($\frac{1}{2}$ in.). Roll it out until it is the same thickness as the sticks, as for tile-making. The surface of the clay must be smooth and level. Press objects such as pebbles, matchsticks, modelling tools, twigs, bones, nails, screws, shells, leaves and feathers into the damp surface, and remove them carefully. Cut the clay to the desired size and let it dry out slowly and completely, then fire in a kiln to an earthenware temperature.

Designs can be cast in reverse in plaster of paris from these clay models, and can also be used as printing blocks. A design can also be cut into the face of a plaster block with a knife after it has set.

Figure 14

14   Clay printing blocks which have been impressed with objects and then fired

15 String block

String print

String, dye or printing ink, printing pad or inking plate, roller, scissors, turps substitute, clean rag, waterproof glue, wood block

Cut a piece of bonded wood to the size required. It should not be less than 12 mm (½ in.) thick.

Put a thick layer of waterproof glue over one surface of the block. Cut the string, bend it to shape and press it into the glue. It can be moved around with the handle of a brush as the glue becomes tacky. The string used must be of an equal thickness over the whole block, otherwise it will not print evenly. For the same reason one piece of string cannot be glued over another. If it is desired to make the lines of string appear to cross each other the string

16 Print made from a string block

17 String mounted on a cardboard tube

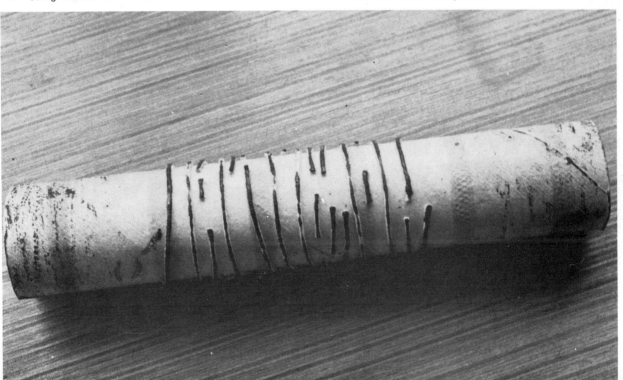

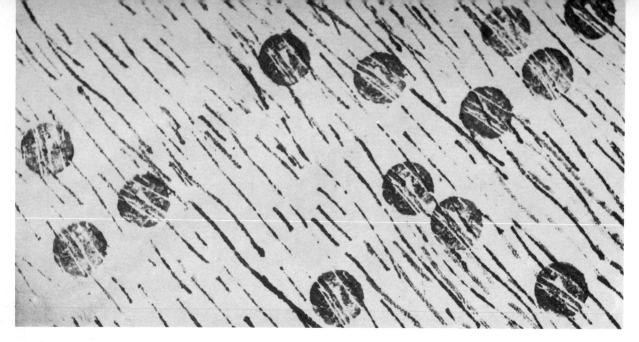

19 Pieces of pipe cleaner fixed to a wood block with water-proof adhesive

18 Print made from string wound round a cardboard tube. Other shapes were printed with the end of a cork

must be cut and the two sections glued on either side of the intersecting line.

The block may be pressed into a dye pad, or rolled up with fabric printing ink from a printing plate. Apart from string, other materials which can be used in a similar way are wire, pipe cleaners, raffia.

These materials can also be attached to some form of roller to give a continuous printing surface—a cardboard tube, section of a broom handle or a rolling pin, for example. The string must be very firmly fixed with a strong glue, and a space should be left at either end of the roller for the hands. Other materials can be attached to the surface of the roller—pieces of felt, rubber, sponge, card, nails, tacks, staples, etc.

Figures 15—20

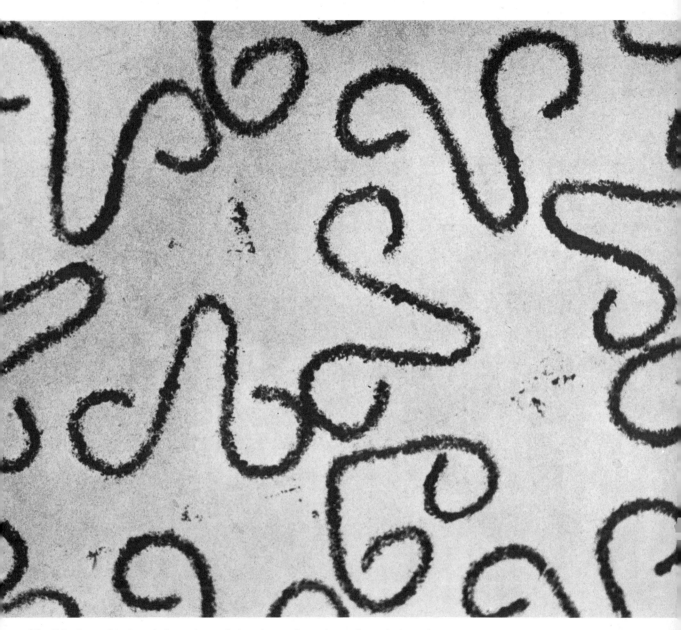

20   Print from a block made from pieces of pipe cleaner shown in previous photograph

Lino and wood cut prints

Woodblock or lino mounted on wood, waterproof glue, dye, spoon, printing pad, newsprint, newspaper, clean rag, wood and lino cutting tools

These are traditional materials for printmaking on fabric and are capable of producing very clear detailed prints. Woodblocks are more expensive but more durable than lino. They are also more difficult to cut. Usually, as in the classroom, the number of prints to be made from the block is relatively small, and therefore lino is the more suitable material.

Tools for lino cutting and wood cutting are of two sorts, those which are fixed into handles and which have to be resharpened regularly,

21   A woodblock and lino mounted on wood, lino cut and wood cutting tools, and mallet

22   Lino block and flocking materials. Flocking powder in a plastic bag, lino block partially inked up with mordant, glass for rolling out mordant and roller

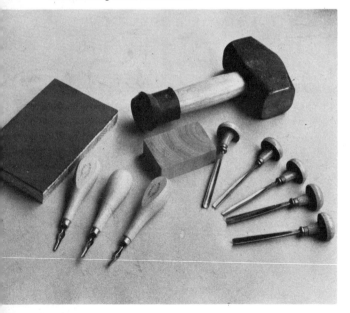

or small blades which are interchangeable in one handle. The latter are cheaper, and when blunted are thrown away and replaced with a new blade. They are more suitable for classroom conditions. Lino is cheap and easy to cut. It must be mounted onto a woodblock the same size as itself before printing. This block should be thick bonded plywood so that it will not warp. Glue the face of the block and the back of the lino together with a strong waterproof adhesive and put them in a press or vice overnight. If the design is prepared on paper beforehand, it can be traced with carbon paper onto the face of the lino. Remember that the design will print in reverse. Cut on a solid table in a good light and away from the body

23 Sun and cloud. A fabric print made from lino and string blocks

for safety's sake. Do not cut either too deeply or too shallow, as the tool may either slip or jam in the block.

Outline the work with a V-shaped tool and clear away the large areas between with U-shaped tools. The edges of the printing areas should never be undercut as this weakens them. Cut back the edges of the block, otherwise these will print off on the cloth if the edges become

inked up. For fabric printing always keep the design bold, as the printing dye tends to fill in the fine spaces. To hold the dye successfully the block should be flocked, as explained on page 9.

When printing, press the face of the block into the printing pad several times, turning it each time to ensure even coverage. The block must be recharged regularly and the pressure on the back of the block when printing must also be regular. For large blocks it is best to strike the back of the block with the handle of a mallet.

Lino need not be cut with lino cutting tools. If the surface is scored with a sharp knife and then bent, it breaks cleanly. Then cut through the canvas at the back of the lino, after which the pieces of lino can be arranged into a design and glued down upon the block. *Figures 21—23*

Progressive lino cut
Lino, woodblock, lino cutting tools, water-proof adhesive, dye, printing pad, spoon, newsprint, newspaper, clean rag

This is sometimes called elimination linocut because the lino is gradually removed as successive colours are printed on top of each other. First cut away those parts of the design which are not to be printed, and will therefore remain the colour of the fabric. Print this over the whole fabric, then clean the block and cut away those parts which are to show the first colour through the next series of prints. Print this over the first series in a different colour, clean the block and cut away further areas. Continue in this way until almost all the lino has been removed. It is usual to start with the

23

24   Progressive lino cut showing four stages of printing

lightest colour and progress to the darkest. Progressive linoprints have a natural unity because each part of the design grows out of the next. Also, printing several dyes on top of each other can give very rich colours. *Figure 24*

24

Screen printing

This is a refinement of the stencil technique, in which all the intricate parts of the stencil are held together by a fine mesh which is stretched over a rectangular frame. It is simple, effective and cheap. The materials required can be bought from suppliers who are listed at the end of this book, but adequate substitutes can in many cases be made. Picture frames, provided they are strong and not warped, can be used. The frame should be smooth. Any nails or projections must be removed. Frames can also easily be made. The wood should be a well seasoned, straight grained soft-wood. The size of the frames can be standardized, which can simplify working conditions and means that only one size of squeegee is required, or a variety of screens may be used to accommodate differences in the sizes of the designs to be printed. Frames can be made to print the whole width of the cloth at once. This means, for a fabric with a width of 915 mm (36 in.) the frame would have to be about 1120 mm (44 in.) long on the inside. A frame with an inside measurement of 460 mm (18 in.) by 300 mm (12 in.) is a useful size. Allowing for the gum paper masking, this will make a repeat of up to 300 mm (12 in.) by 250 mm (10 in.). The wood should be about 40 mm (1½ in.) by 25 mm (1 in.) thick and should be varnished to help prevent warping. The four pieces can be joined at the corners with metal brackets.

Silk, nylon and *Terylene* are strong and elastic, give very even printing and fine detail, but are expensive. Cotton organdie will not stand very rough handling, but is cheap and

25 Some materials required for screen printing: screen, squeegee, organdie, drawing pins, stapler, gumstrip paper, scissors, dye in a plastic bowl, clean rag and newspaper

adequate for short runs of material. The gauze must be stretched tightly across the frame and fixed to it with staples, drawing pins or strong waterproof glue, or a combination of these. The warp and weft of the organdie must run parallel to the sides of the frame. When using drawing pins or staples, tack down one side at intervals of about 25 mm (1 in.), then pull the cloth firmly but gently to the opposite side of the frame and tack it down, starting in the middle and working towards the corners. Do the same with the other two sides, then trim off the surplus cloth at the edges. The screen must be stretched taut, otherwise a sharp print will not be obtained. Wet the cloth on both sides. This will cause it to shrink and will tighten it. While it is still wet, mask the outside of the frame with wide brown paper gumstrip so that a 'window' is left in the middle of the screen through which the colour will pass. The masked area should be 100 mm (4 in.) at either end and 25 mm (1 in.) wide at the sides

27 The squeegee in the printing frame. A large nail at either end of the squeegee will prevent it falling into the dye. A stick under the screen, when it is not in use, will keep it off the surface of the table

26 A home-made screen of varnished wood joined at the corners with metal brackets

of the screen. The area at each end is where the dye and squeegee remain between prints. Make sure that the outside and inside edges of the frame are also covered with gumstrip to prevent the colour seeping through when printing. When the screen is dry, varnish over the whole frame, including the brown paper, inside and out, except for the rectangle in the middle. This will make the entire screen waterproof, will facilitate washing, and will allow the squeegee to run smoothly over the screen. Allow the varnish to dry thoroughly before using the screen.

Some of the many varied ways of making

the screen stencils will be described later, but it should be realized that any material can be used to make the stencil, provided that it will block areas of the screen to prevent the dye passing through. Also it must not be dissolved by the dye pigment. Varnish, lacquer, oil paint, wax, shellac, rubber solution, PVA, photographic gelatine, paper, string, are some of the materials which can be used. These can be applied to the screen by painting, splashing, spraying, rubbing, stencilling and printing. Each material will have qualities, advantages and disadvantages, of its own. Some will dry quickly, some slowly. Some will be removable and some irremovable from the screen. The important thing is to experiment and, if it works, use it.

28 A small hand window-cleaner makes a good squeegee for small screens

29 Some very useful, though not essential, equipment for screen-printing: steam iron, timer, ultra violet lamp and hairdryer

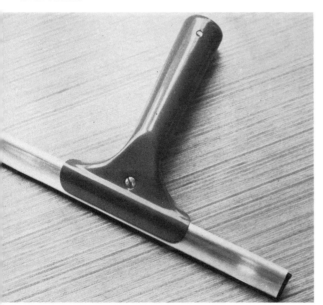

The various stencils to be used on the screen, which are described later, can be made more permanent by coating them with varnish. Brush a mixture of varnish slightly diluted with turps substitute over the whole stencil, then clean out the open spaces from the reverse side of the screen with a soft cloth slightly damped with turps substitute.

The squeegee, which pushes dye through the screen, is made of a hard rubber or plastic strip sandwiched between two pieces of wood to form a handle. For small screens a window cleaner's squeegee can be used. This is easier for young children because it is light to handle. The squeegee should be slightly smaller than the inside width of the frame, and it must also

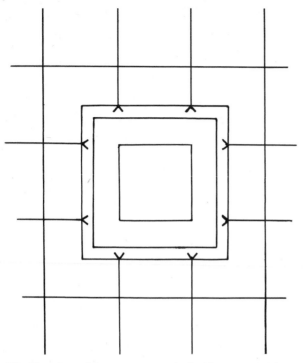

at the ends. The edges of the screen are marked with four arrows, and these are aligned with the threads on the fabric to give a correct register (see figure 30).

The most convenient colours for screen printing, because they are very simple to prepare, are pigment dyes. These can be obtained under various trade names, but are basically the same. They consist of a white emulsion called the binder, to which is added a small amount of dye. The binder can be obtained in 22.5 kg (50 lb) containers, and this is the most economical way to use it.

The dyes can be obtained in a very wide range of colours, including gold, silver and white. They can be used on natural and synthetic materials, but are not effective on wool or velvet.

To prepare the dye put enough binder for the job in hand into a jar or plastic basin.

30 The edges of the screen are marked with arrows and these are aligned with the threads on the fabric to give correct registration

31 Print alternate squares of the pattern in the order indicated. This reduces the risk of marking off adjacent wet prints

1	11	2	12	3
13	4	14	5	15
6	16	7	17	8
18	9	19	10	20

be wider than the design on the screen.

The fabric on which the design is to be screen printed must be pinned down to the backcloth to prevent any movement during printing. In order to obtain a correct register, a line should be drawn on the backcloth parallel to one long edge of the table, and one selvage of the fabric to be printed is pinned against this. All other measurements are taken from this line when squaring up the cloth. Points should be marked on all edges of the cloth, and thread stretched across and pinned or taped down

These containers should have an airtight lid, so that the dye may be stored for further use if required. As the dyes are powerful, add only a small amount to the binder at a time, and stir it in well. Try a spot of colour on the corner of the cloth to be printed. It will dry out a lighter shade, and this must always be taken into consideration when making the dyes. The emulsion should be like a smooth cream with no lumps or small pieces of dye in it.

When printing it helps to have two people working on one screen, especially if it is large. Pour the colour along the masked area at one end. Pull this with a squeegee held at an angle of 45°, with an even pressure, firmly and smoothly to the other end of the screen. Do not stop halfway across, as this will leave a distinct line on the print. Before printing on cloth, trial prints should be made on paper. The number of times the squeegee is pulled across for each print depends on the consistency of the colour and the thickness of the fabric and density of print required.

When printing, do not place the screen over a wet, newly printed section. To avoid this, print alternate repeats and then return to fill in the intervening spaces later. The newly printed areas should be covered with newspaper. A hairdryer can be useful in speeding the drying process. If the work is suspended even for a short while, the dye will start to dry in the screen; it will then have to be washed out and the screen dried before printing can recommence.

After printing, allow the cloth to dry, then in order to fix the pigment dye iron the back with the heat set at the correct temperature for the fabric.

Paper pick-up stencil

Screen, squeegee, dye, spoon, craft knife, scissors, newspaper, newsprint, clean rag

Cut or tear out shapes from newspaper. Arrange these on a sheet of newsprint. Put the screen over them, pour the dye into the screen at one end and squeegee it across. Raise the screen and it will be found that the colour has penetrated between the pieces, and at the same time has picked up the pieces of paper which will now remain attached to the screen for further printing. Although the original design may be simple, by overprinting this design in the same or another colour, more complex shapes may be obtained. The first

32   A paper pick-up stencil print. The design was overprinted in the same colour after turning the screen once at 90° to the first print

print must be dry before a second is made on top of it.

With paper pick-up it is a simple matter to remove or add pieces of paper to the design in the course of printing. If it is desired to change the colour but to keep the original design, the pieces must be removed and the screen washed and dried. To reset the pieces, put them in their correct positions on the first print, then squeegee over them with the new colour. Any pieces which fail to stick to the screen can be held with a small spot of gum.

This method will give a negative design. For a positive design take a piece of thin paper. Cut out shapes through which the colour must pass. Turn the screen underside upwards and tape this paper to the screen. See that the surrounding area is properly masked off with gumstrip paper and varnished. *Figure 32*

33 Screen print made by using leaves as a stencil

shapes, but this can be an attractive feature of the design. *Figures 33, 34*

34 Sacking material used as a stencil. As with paper pick-up, it is held to the screen by the adhesive nature of the dye

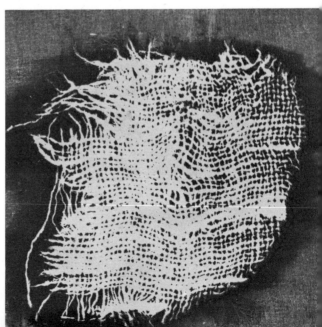

Stencils from leaves and other materials
Screen, squeegee, dye, scissors, newspaper, newsprint, clean rag

As with paper pick-up stencils it is possible to attach to the screen many thin, lightweight materials such as leaves, pressed flowers, feathers, string, raffia, confetti, sand, flour and other powders. Place them on the surface to be printed, put the screen on top and pull the dye across with the squeegee. One pull is usually sufficient, but if some parts of the stencil do not adhere, a small amount of gum rubbed through the screen will hold them.

With fairly thick objects it may be found that a halo of dye forms around the edges of the

30

Profilm

Organdie or silk screen only, squeegee, profilm, craft knife, cutting board, drawing pins, iron, dye, spoon, newspaper, clean rag, methylated spirits

Profilm is more durable than paper stencils and is very effective for making intricate and sharp-edged designs. It is an amber semi-transparent lacquer film attached to a backing sheet of tissue paper. This is pinned over a prepared drawing. The shiny lacquer side of

35 *Profilm* was used to make the screen print in brown and deep grey on a white cotton fabric

36 The stencil for this design was cut from *Profilm* and printed with *Printex* in orange-red on an orange background

the profilm must be upwards and the original design will show through it. Cut over the lines with a sharp knife to penetrate the top layer of lacquer but not the underlying tissue paper. This requires a certain amount of skill, and it is wise to practice on spare pieces of profilm before attempting a proper design. When the shapes have been cut, peel away those parts of the top layer of lacquer which will not be required, leaving the tissue paper below intact.

Put the profilm, shiny side up, onto a piece of paper. Lay the screen over this so that stencil and gauze are in direct contact. Put another sheet of paper on top of the gauze, then pass a warm iron over the surface. This will melt the lacquer beneath which will adhere to the screen. When this happens it will turn a darker shade of brown. Turn the screen over and peel off the backing paper. If parts of the profilm have not adhered, iron them again. The stencil is now ready for printing. Profilm can be removed from the screen by soaking in methylated spirits.
Figures 35, 36

Colour plate 2   Screen sprint made by putting leaves on to a photographic gelatine screen

Wax stencils

Screen, squeegee, dye, spoon, wax heater, paraffin wax or candles, brush, PVA (Polyvinyl Acetate), hot water, iron, newsprint, clean rag

Prepare the wax by melting down the candles or, if in block form, by cutting the block into small pieces, and melting these in a double saucepan. The wax should be hot and must spread smoothly. Lumpy wax will impede the passage of the squeegee. Any such thick areas should be scraped smooth with the edge of a ruler when the wax has cooled.

Lean the screen against a sill or frame of a window or some convenient object, so that the light shines through the mesh. It will then be possible to see the waxed areas clearly. Remember that the parts which are painted out with wax will not print, only the open areas of the screen. If all or part of the wax needs to be removed, put the screen on a pad of newspaper with more newspaper on top and melt the wax out with a hot iron.

To obtain a negative of this design, paint the entire screen, including the waxed areas, with PVA mixed with water (to the consistency of a thin cream) which will become insoluble in water when dry. Make sure that the screen mesh is completely filled. When the PVA is dry, put the screen under hot water. This will melt out the wax and carry away the PVA which is on top of it, leaving the remainder of the PVA to form a reversed stencil of the design. Allow the screen to dry before printing.
Figure 37

37   The stencil for this screen print was made by brushing hot wax direct onto the organdie

Wax crayon on screen

Screen, squeegee, dye, candle or wax crayon, PVA, iron, brush, water, clean rag, black drawing ink, pen, cartridge paper

The design may be prepared actual size on white paper. It should be drawn in strong black lines so that it will show clearly through the screen. Put the drawing on a flat surface and the screen over it, so that the design can be seen through the gauze. Trace over the design with the wax crayon or candle. Press firmly as the wax must fill the mesh of the screen.

The screen will now give a negative print as illustrated in figure 38. At this stage if the wax is to be removed from the screen, put the screen on a pad of newspaper with more news-

Colour plate 3   Screen print made from a letrafilm positive

38   The stencil was made by drawing directly onto the screen with a wax crayon

paper on top and melt it out with a hot iron, or put the screen in hot water.

In order to obtain a positive print, paint over the entire screen, including the wax, with a mixture of PVA and water. When the PVA is completely dry, immerse the screen in hot water which will melt out the waxed areas, but will leave the PVA intact to act as the stencil. When the screen is dry, a positive print can be made.
Figure 38

Wax rubbing on screen
Materials as above

The wax crayon can be used to make a rubbing on the screen. Put the screen over any interesting raised textured surfaces. Make sure that the surface to be rubbed is as clean as possible. Rub firmly over the gauze so that strong areas of wax are built up to form the stencil. Then the screen is ready for printing.
Figure 39

34

39 A screen print made from a wax rubbing of a string collage.
The screen was rubbed over the string, then moved slightly and rubbed again

Wax stencil using a soldering-iron

*Screen, squeegee, dye, spoon, paraffin wax,
wax heater, brush, newspaper, soldering-iron,
clean rag, iron*

Paint wax over the entire screen. This is best
done with the screen leaning at an angle of 45°
against a window frame so that the light is
behind it; it is then possible to see if there are
any pinholes in the wax. Put the wax on

thinly, because lumps will impede the movement of the squeegee. These can, however,
be smoothed down afterwards with the edge
of a ruler. Stand the frame in a cool place to
harden the wax. To make the stencil, place the
screen on a sheet of paper on which the design
has been drawn in strong outline, so that it
shows clearly through the wax. Draw over the
design with the tip of the soldering-iron. The
iron must be hot enough to melt the wax, but

35

not so hot that it burns through the screen, and for the same reason it must be kept moving. The slower the soldering-iron is moved the wider will be the melted line. When the wax is cool the stencil is ready for printing.
Figure 40

In figure 40 it can be seen that large areas of wax have melted at corners and intersections of the lines, where the iron has paused momentarily.

40 A screen print from a wax stencil. The design was melted into the wax with a soldering-iron

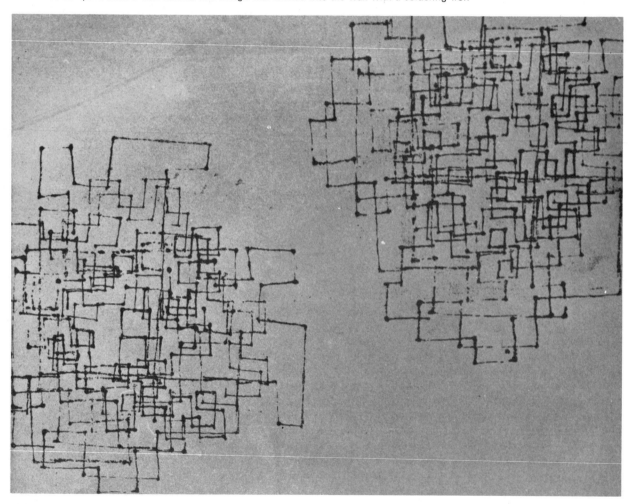

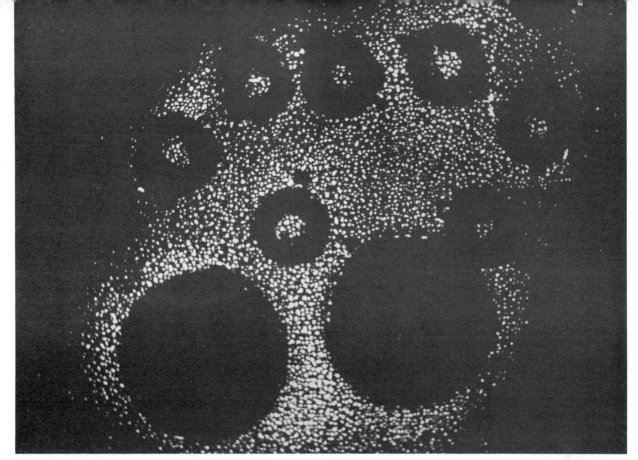

41　The stencil for this screen print was made by spraying thin varnish over metal washers which were placed on the screen

Sprayed stencil

Screen, squeegee, dye, spoon, spraygun or fixative mouthspray, newspaper, clean rag

The stencil can be made by spraying a liquid onto the screen. This liquid must be thin enough to pass through a spraygun without blocking it, and it must also be insoluble when dry in water based dyes. Varnish or shellac can be used. The material can be sprayed onto the screen with a paint spray operated by compressed air, or with a fixative mouth spray.

Areas of the screen can be masked off with various objects to make a pattern. Light materials such as cut paper, leaves, feathers, or anything which might be blown away by the air from the paint spray, must be attached to the screen with water based gum. This can be washed out later.
Figure 41

Mixed colour screen print

Screen, squeegee, dye, newspaper, newsprint, clean rag

It is usual to screen print only one colour at a time. It is, however, possible to print two or more colours with one pull of the squeegee. Put a separate spoonful of each colour in the space at the end of the screen in the order required, then pull them across in the usual way. The colours will merge to make intermediate shades where they join. If isolated parts of the design are to be printed in different colours, the dye can be pushed through the screen with a brush, rag, or even with the fingers.
Figure 42

42 A mixed colour screen print using a cut-up paper doyley as the stencil

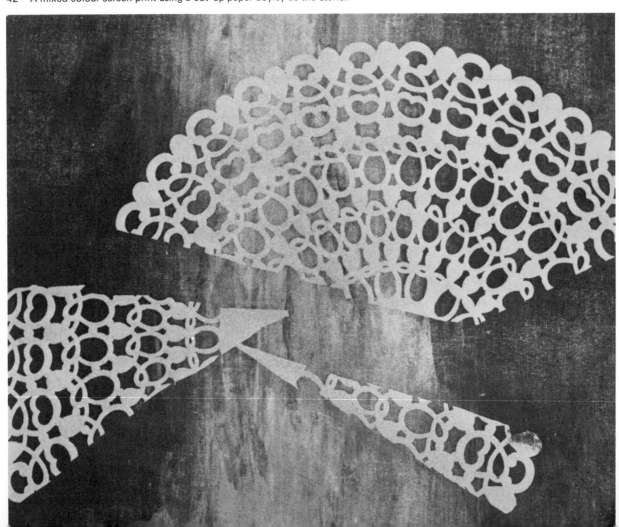

Photographic stencils

Some of the most interesting and efficient ways of making stencils for screen printing are by using photographic methods. With them it is possible to reproduce almost any sort of design from hand drawn or photographic sources, and these can be very intricate.

A cheap and simple photographic stencil can be made from gelatine and potassium bichromate. Stir 1 part granulated photographic gelatine powder into 10 parts warm water, heat gradually but do not boil. When ready the solution should be like thin cream. Apply this while hot to the screen with a large brush. Tilt the screen at an angle so that the liquid runs on smoothly and collects at the bottom of the frame where it can be removed with a cloth or dry brush. Make sure that the entire screen is covered. It is best to give it three separate coats, allowing each coat to dry before applying the next. This will ensure a good even coverage. To make the gelatine light-sensitive, it must finally be given a coat of potassium bichromate, but this should be left until just before the screen is to be used. Potassium bichromate is an orange powder which should be stored in a dark dry place. Mix 2.5 cc of potassium bichromate to 100 cc of water. This can be kept as a stock solution. Wash this quickly over the entire gelatine surface of the screen with a large soft brush, then put the screen immediately into a completely light-tight cupboard, drawer or darkroom to dry, because it will now be light-sensitive. When it is dry it is ready for use. On exposure to light the combination of gelatine and potassium bichromate will become insoluble in water. If parts of the screen are pro-tected from the light the gelatine will remain soluble and can be washed away, thus forming the stencil.

Photo-stencil materials are especially manufactured for screen-printing, and some suppliers of these are given at the end of this book. They will provide full information about their products on request. These stencils give clearer images than gelatine, but are all more expensive. The best known of these materials is *Seriset*. This is a plastic emulsion which is mixed with potassium bichromate and is applied to the screen with an emulsion coating trough, after which it must be stored in the dark. It is exposed to the light and then washed out in the same way as with gelatine stencils.

The light source for the photographic screen may be daylight or artificial light. The disadvantage of daylight is that it varies in intensity, and this means that the exposure time cannot be standardized. Bright sunlight will harden the screen in a few minutes, while on a dull day it may take an hour or more to obtain the same result. The artificial light can be from photoflood lamps, carbon arc or ultra violet lamps. Carbon arcs are expensive and not safe for use with young people. Photofloods are cheap, convenient, and have the advantage that they can be used for other photographic work, but they are slow. An ultra violet lamp is fairly cheap and it is quick. It is also a 'cold' light, which is important because the temperature on the screen surface should not exceed 30°C (85°F). The following table gives approximate exposure times for various light sources:

sunlight	5 minutes
bright daylight	10 minutes

dull daylight	1 to 2 hours
300W floodlamp at 600 mm (24 in.)	1½ hours
ultra-violet lamp at 450 mm (18 in.)	10 minutes

Figures 43 and 44 show exploded views of two methods of illuminating the light-sensitive stencil. Figure 43 shows the light, either natural or artificial, coming from above and passing through a sheet of plate glass. Between the glass and the light-sensitive surface of the screen is the positive (see below), on which there is an opaque design.

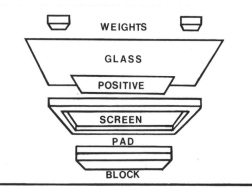

43 An arrangement for transferring the design from the positive to the photographic screen using a light from above

The glass is held in close contact with the positive and screen by lead weights. A padded block presses from below against the underside of the screen, and the assembly rests upon a table, windowsill or other suitable surface. Figure 44 illustrates a light box using an ultra violet lamp. In this case the light is below, and the positive and screen face downwards onto the glass. The weights are on the

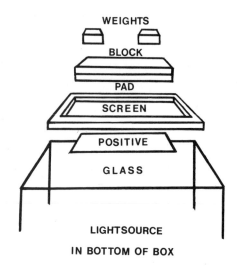

44 An arrangement for transferring a design from the positive to a photographic screen by using a light box

back of the padded block so that screen, positive and glass are pressed together.

The design which is used to make the photographic stencil, whether it is a solid object, a painting in opaque ink on a transparent paper, or an image on photographic paper, is called the positive. The simplest positive with which to make a photographic stencil is an opaque object such as a leaf, flower or feather, or a pair of scissors. If these are placed on a light-sensitive screen they will stop the light from reaching and hardening the sensitive emulsion. The area surrounding the object will, however, receive the light and will be hardened. When the screen is sprayed with warm water those parts of the screen protected from the light will be dissolved, giving a clear stencil image of the object.

To make a painted positive, the design for the stencil is made in opaque ink or paint on transparent paper, plastic or glass. It is most important that the design should be really opaque. To test this, hold the design up to a very bright light to see whether the light penetrates the opaque areas. Positives can also be made by photographic means using photographic lith paper. These, and other forms of positive, are described in the following sections of this book.

Lacquer and gelatine screen
Gelatine screen, lacquer, squeegee, potassium bichromate, brush, dye, spoon, newspaper, clean rag, light source

Prepare the screen with gelatine alone as described on page 39. Paint the design with lacquer on the underside of the screen. When this has dried, cover the entire underside of the screen, including the design, with liquid potassium bichromate. This should be applied as a thin wash with a large, soft brush. Tilt the screen at an angle of 45°. Start at the top of the screen and work from left to right and downwards until the screen is completely covered. Do not flood the liquid on, otherwise it may penetrate the gelatine and creep under the lacquer. Put the screen underside upwards under the light source and leave it until the potassium bichromate has turned from yellow to deep brown. The length of time this takes will depend on the strength of the light. Wash the screen in warm water. The gelatine beneath the lacquer and the lacquer itself will

45   Moth and flame design in three colours printed with three lacquer gelatine screens

wash away. The gelatine in the areas affected by the potassium bichromate will not wash away and will form the stencil. Put the screen onto a sheet of newspaper and gently remove the excess water and any particles of gelatine remaining inside the stencil area by dabbing with a soft clean cloth. Allow the screen to dry and it is then ready for printing.
Figure 45

Dry transfer stencils

Screen, squeegee, gelatine, potassium bichromate, gelatine heater, brushes, dye, spoon, newspaper, clean rag, dry transfers, light source

The many signs, symbols and textures in the form of dry transfers can be used for stencils for screen printing. They may be attached directly to the screen in the conventional way, and provided they are rubbed down well will survive many printings. The image will, of course, be a negative one; that is, the background will print and the transfer will remain unprinted. To reverse this and to make a much more durable stencil, cover the screen thoroughly with gelatine. When the gelatine is completely dry, apply the transfers and rub them down well. Put a wash of potassium bichromate over the entire screen, including the lettering, with a large soft brush. Place the screen transfer side up under the light until the potassium bichromate has turned brown. Then immerse the screen in warm water. The unexposed gelatine beneath the dry transfer will dissolve, leaving a clear open stencil.

Figure 46

46   Screen print made with a dry transfer stencil

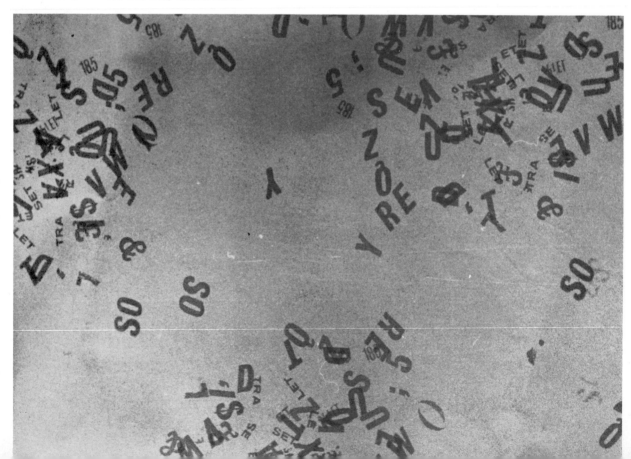

Objects on a photographic screen

Screen, squeegee, plate glass, light source, pressure pad, potassium bichromate and gelatine, or other photo-sensitive emulsions, brush, dye, spoon, clean rag

The objects to be reproduced must be fairly flat, such as leaves, feathers, scissors, string, lace, netting, doylies, twigs, bones, wire. If some light penetrates the objects they can be rendered opaque by coating them with opaque ink or paint.

47 This screen print was made from a gelatine potassium bichromate stencil. Leaves were put on the light-sensitive screen, which was then exposed to daylight

If the screen (which has been made light-sensitive) is to be exposed to a light from above, put the pad on a table or other suitable area, and put the screen underside upwards over the pad. Place the objects to be copied on the screen and put the plate glass on top of them. The weight of the glass will press the objects into the pad and will thus ensure a good contact with the screen. Some weights around the outside of the glass will give extra pressure. If the light source is below the screen, as described on page 40, then the objects, screen and pad will be inverted on the glass and the weights will be put on the back of the pad. After exposure put the screen in warm water. This will wash out the unexposed areas of the emulsion.
Figure 47

Opaque positive designs

Prepared photographic screen, squeegee, tracing paper, transparent plastic sheet, Koda-trace or glass, black drawing ink, opaque paint or ink, brush or pen, light source, pad, plate-glass, dye, spoon, clean rag

To prepare opaque designs for photographic screens, use can be made of any opaque media such as black drawing ink, poster paint or opaque ink. This is applied to the transparent base—sheet of glass, transparent plastic sheet, tracing paper, or *Kodatrace*. It may be applied by any means, for example with a brush or pen, or by spraying, splashing, dribbling, etc. Check to see that the design is opaque by holding it up to a strong light. If light shows through, give the design an extra coat. Wax can be applied to the transparent material by any means—drawing, rubbing, dripping—then the

43

opaque ink is painted over the wax to produce a resist pattern. Prepare the photographic screen as described previously, and store it in a completely light-tight drawer, cupboard, box, or darkroom. To make the photographic stencil on the screen, place the prepared opaque positive design face downwards in direct contact with the sensitive surface of the photographic screen. Arrange the glass and pad as described on page 40 and then expose to the light source. Wash out the screen in warm water and allow it to dry before printing. *Figure 48, 49*

Scratched positive
Materials as above

Paint over the surface of a piece of glass or transparent plastic with some form of opaque ink or paint. It will need more than one coat to make it truly opaque. When this is dry, scratch a design into the surface with a sharp point such as a compass or etching needle. This will produce a fine clear line like an etching. To produce a reversed etched line, scratch directly into the surface of the transparent plastic sheet, then rub a thick black ink into the lines. Wipe the surface of the plastic clear with a clean rag, leaving the ink in the scratches. These positives can then be used to make a photographic screen.

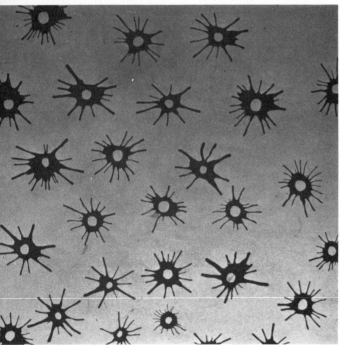

Opaque paper designs

Prepared photographic screen, squeegee, opaque paper, handcut masking film or Letrafilm, scissors, craft knife, board for cutting, rubber solution, tracing paper, transparent plastic sheet, Kodatrace or glass, light source, dye, spoon, clean rag

Any opaque material can be used to make a positive for the preparation of photographic screens. If cut paper designs are used, the paper need not be black, providing it is thick enough to stop the light. Attach it to the transparent base with rubber solution. The advantage of rubber solution is that the pieces of paper can be lifted off and replaced elsewhere if required.

The dry stencil material called *Letrafilm* can be used to make paper positives. Besides the black *Letrafilm* the red and amber sheets are also photo-opaque. This is because they are photo-safe colours which eliminate the ultra-violet light which hardens the photographic emulsion. Draw the shapes required on the back of a sheet of *Letrafilm*, then cut them out with scissors or craft knife. Peel off the backing paper and press the shapes into place on the transparent base. When the design is complete, put it face downwards into contact with the light-sensitive surface of the screen and expose to the light source.

Figure 50

50   The positive for this photographic screen print was made by cutting shapes from red *Letrafilm* and fixing it to tracing paper

Oil paper positive

Photographic screen, squeegee, oiled paper positive, light source, dye, spoon, clean rag

A photographic screen can be made from any design in opaque ink or paint on paper. It must be remembered, however, that the back of the paper should be blank. The exposure time will be longer because the light has to penetrate a greater density of material, but if paraffin wax or some other greasy substance is rubbed over the paper this will make it more transparent.

Screens can be made in this way from prints produced by a photo-copier. The image to be copied can also be a lino cut or leaf print.

TP paper positive

Kodak TP Paper, *developer, fixative, photographic dishes, dark-room with other materials as required for conventional photographic enlarging and developing*

TP Paper is a translucent light-sensitive material of much more contrast than conventional photographic paper. It breaks the image up into areas that are completely black and opaque or completely transparent. *TP Paper* can be used like ordinary photographic printing paper and images can be printed on it by contact printing or enlarging. The image can be from a photograph or it can be a photogram. A special developer is used for this paper. The procedure for mixing up the developer is simple, and provided the manufacturer's instructions are followed, will give excellent results. This paper has a wide latitude so that times of exposure do not have to be very exact.

When the paper has been developed and fixed and dried, it is ready to be used like any

other positive design to make the photographic stencil.

Photograms on TP paper

Materials as above

To make photograms on *TP Paper*, as with conventional photographic printing paper, it is not essential to use an enlarger. Images can be made on the paper by placing objects directly on it to impede the light, and these can then be exposed to ordinary artifical light. Images can also be made by projecting from an enlarger. Materials which are put into the negative carrier of the enlarger cannot be very big, for example, thread, hair, crumpled cellophane, ink, liquid detergent, seeds. Large objects such as jewellery, keys, scissors, leaves, feathers, bones, cut paper, lace, doylies, can be placed directly on the surface of the paper.

51   This photogram on *TP Paper* shows the variety of size obtainable from the same objects. Some pins were placed on the *TP Paper*, others were put into the negative carrier of the enlarger

After exposure to the light for the required time, develop and fix according to the manufacturer's instructions.
Figure 51

Photomontage positives

Old TP Paper *positives, scissors, tracing paper, transparent plastic sheet,* Kodatrace *or glass, rubber solution*

Cut up old *TP Paper* and arrange the pieces upon a transparent base. When these have been combined to make a suitable design, stick them down with small spots of rubber solution. The completed photomontage is then used as a positive to make a photographic stencil as previously described.
Figure 52

52   A positive made from a variety of old *TP Paper* positives which were cut up and arranged on a sheet of glass as an abstract design

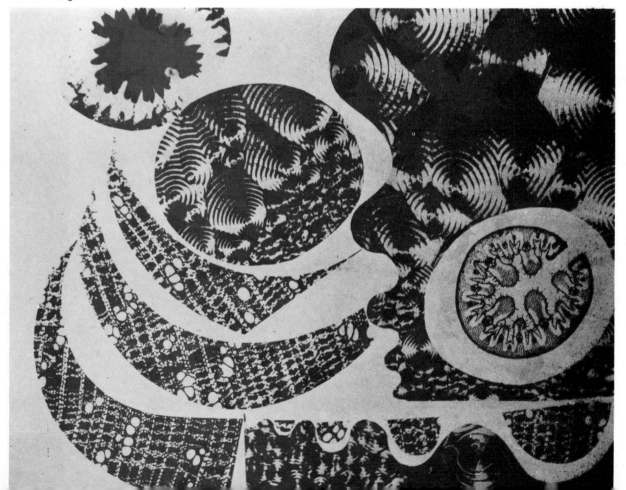

Wax Resist (Batik)

This consists of the application of hot wax to the cloth which is subsequently dyed. The fabric is patterned with wax and then immersed in a cold dye, which is repelled by the wax but absorbed into the fabric in the unwaxed areas.

A heater is required to melt the wax. A gas ring or electric hotplate, preferably with an enclosed element, are the most useful. The wax container can be a double saucepan, or a gluepot with surrounding water jacket. Paraffin wax in block form is cut up and melted in the container of the heater. If many people, as in a classroom, are to use the wax at the same time,

53 Batik of a heraldic eagle in red and purple *Procion M* dye on white calico

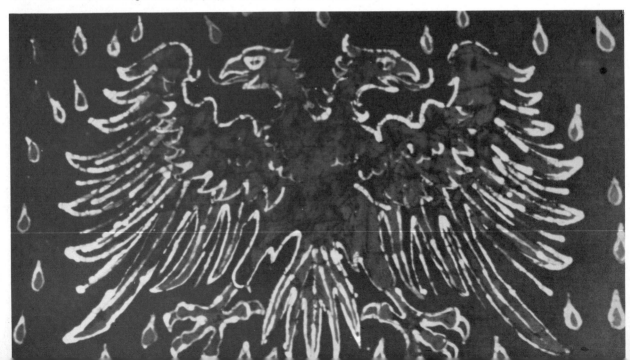

it is best to distribute it in tins, such as small baked bean tins. The wax can be kept hot by putting the tins on top of others of the same size, each of which contains a lighted candle. Plenty of holes must be punched in the sides of the lower tins to let in the air, otherwise the candles will not burn.

The fabric must be thoroughly washed before use to remove substances which may prevent the cloth from fully absorbing the dye. The best materials are those containing natural fibres. Artificial fibres, non-iron, crease-resistant, drip-dry materials, are not suitable as they do not absorb the dye easily.

Cover the table top and surrounding floor area with plenty of newspaper. The cloth may be laid flat on the newspaper on the table, or may be stretched on a wood frame. If it is put directly onto the newspaper it will stick to it,

as the wax penetrates the cloth, and when it is removed the wax will crack. If it does stick to the cloth to any great extent, it is best to put cloth and newspaper in the dye together. To avoid this complication it is easy to construct a frame to the size of the cloth required. This merely requires four wood battens which should be neatly joined at the corners. The edges of the cloth are fixed to the frame with drawing pins or staples. These edges can be trimmed before hemming on completion of the batik. It is necessary to leave a good margin around the original design for this purpose.

If the wax does crack, dye will enter the cracks giving a mottled effect. It is a common practice to exaggerate this by squeezing the waxed cloth before dyeing. To avoid excessive cracking, add a small amount of beeswax to the paraffin wax, which will make it less brittle.

54   Detail of eagle batik showing an area of cracked and scratched wax

55 Some useful equipment for batik: electric hotplate, double saucepan, electric wax heater, candles, brushes and tin cans for holding wax

The design may be drawn lightly in pencil on the cloth, or a drawing may be made in strong black outline on white paper. This can then be put beneath the cloth, and provided that the material is not very thick it will show clearly through. The wax can be applied in many different ways, but it should always be hot enough to penetrate through the cloth, other-

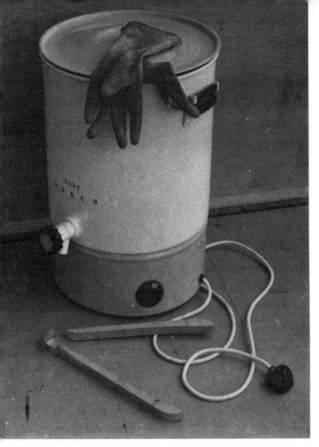

56 An electric boiler is useful for washing, dyeing or boiling off wax from the fabric in batik work

wise the dye will get beneath the wax and the resist will not be efficient. To make more certain of the resist the design may be made on both sides of the material. The wax can be applied by dripping from a lighted candle, rubbing with wax crayon, painting, dipping, or printing with such materials as card, wood-blocks, nails, etc. A tjanting can be used (see page 55).

Accidental drops of wax can be removed from the fabric by scraping, then ironing them between pieces of newspaper, or by rubbing with rag dipped in paraffin. To avoid unwanted splashes, cover as much of the cloth as possible with newspaper.

The fabric may be dyed in any large container, providing these are not of a corrosive material. Measure out enough cold water to cover the fabric to be dyed. Mix the dye in a separate small container according to the manufacturer's instructions. Pour the prepared dye into the large container of water and stir it well. Immerse the cloth quickly and leave it until the required shade is obtained. Remember that the colour will look darker when the material is wet, and also that there will be a loss of colour after rinsing. Instead of immersing the whole cloth, certain parts only can be dyed by dipping, or dye may be applied to certain areas with a brush.

After dyeing, spread the fabric out flat on newspapers so that it dries evenly. A large sheet of polythene beneath the newspapers will protect the table or floor. When dry, the fabric may be rewaxed and dyed again in another colour. It is usual to start with the lighter colours and work towards the darker ones. When the work is complete the wax is removed. A certain amount can be picked or scraped off, then the cloth is put into hot water with a little detergent. The wax will rise to the surface, and when the water is cool it can be collected for further use. Several separate treatments in hot water will remove most of the wax. Finally, iron the material between sheets of newspaper. Do not allow wax to go down the sink outlet as this can block it.

Wax splashing and dripping

Candles or melted wax, heater, brush, wood frame, cold dye, rubber gloves, iron, newspaper

Wax can be splashed and dripped as well as painted onto the cloth. Pin the fabric to a wood frame. A large empty picture frame will do, or a frame can be made by joining four pieces of wood together at the corners. To make long splashes, hold the frame vertically and let the wax drop from the brush or lighted candle so that it falls and runs in elongated shapes. The frame can at the same time be turned to vary the design. The cloth is dyed, and can be re-waxed when dry and dyed again. Plenty of newspaper should be spread over the floor and tables to catch the wax which misses its mark.

Figure 57

57   Wax was splashed on the cloth, which was dyed in two colours

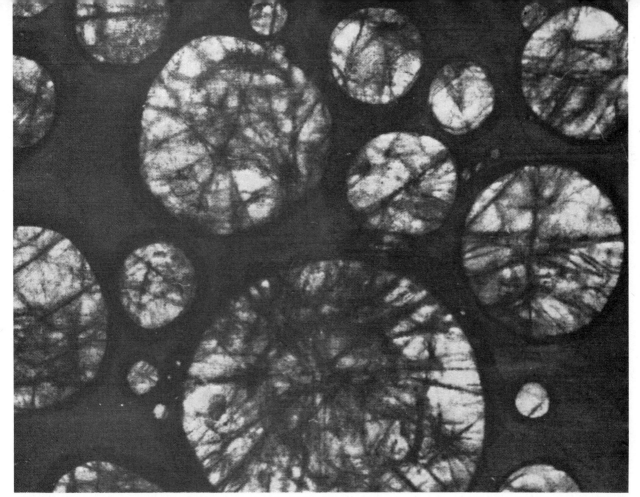

58 Wax was poured onto the cloth from a spoon, and when hard was cracked by squeezing in the hand. The dye has penetrated the cracks to give the veined effect

Wax veining

Paraffin wax, candles, heater, brush, cold dye, rubber gloves, iron, newspaper, clean rag

The well-known veined effect is one of the attractions of wax resist. To obtain it, use the brittle paraffin wax. The wax must be hot enough to penetrate the cloth well. It must then be allowed to cool. The best way to do this is to put it under a cold tap. When the wax is hard, squeeze it in the hands, which will break it into thousands of hairlike cracks. When the material is immersed in dye, the colour will penetrate the cloth between the cracks.

Figures 58, 59

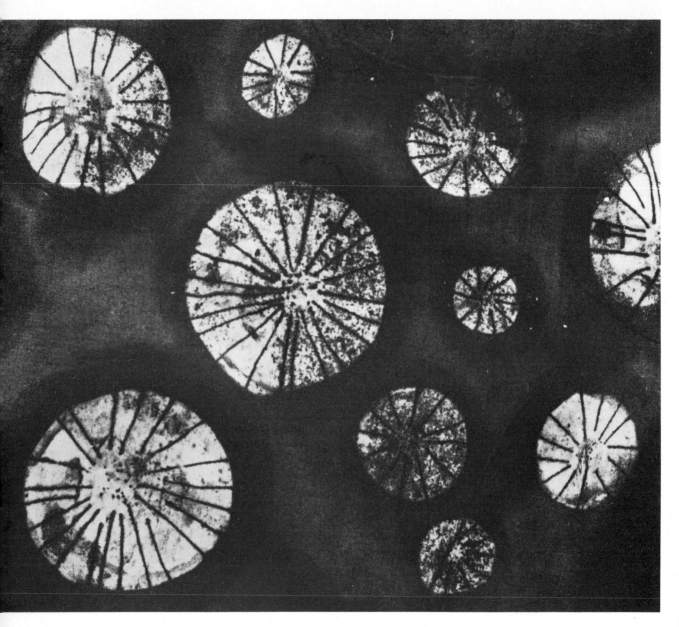

59 Circles of wax applied to the cloth with a spoon were scratched and stippled with a compass point

The tjanting

Paraffin wax, heater, double saucepan, tjanting, cold water dye, bowl, rubber gloves, newspaper, iron

The tjanting has been used in SE Asia for the production of batik for many centuries. It comes in various shapes and sizes, but basically consists of a metal tube or container tapering to a fine spout. This container is attached to a wooden handle. The container is filled with hot wax which runs out in an even stream from the spout. Skill should be acquired by practising on paper before proceeding to a proper design on cloth. The most difficult problem for a beginner is to control the flow of wax as desired. Dip the tjanting into the hot wax, and on lifting it out put a small pad of paper or cloth over the spout to stop the wax from escaping until the tjanting is in contact with the fabric. Tjantings can be obtained with spouts of various sizes to make fine or thick lines.
Figures 60, 61

60   A tjanting and wax printing blocks attached to sticks

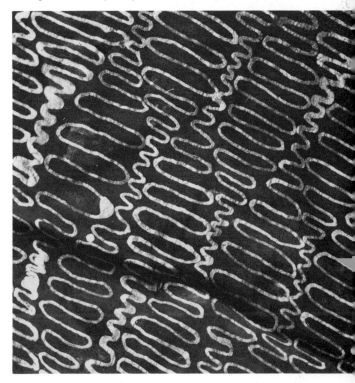

61   Tjanting design. A continuous wavy line pattern made by trailing wax from a tjanting over the cloth and then dyeing

Wax printing from blocks

Paraffin wax, heater, double saucepan, cold dye, bowl, rubber gloves, newspaper, iron

The tjap is a traditional wax printing block used by the people of SE Asia. It is made of thin sheets of metal set vertically to form a pattern. This is dipped into hot wax and printed off onto cloth which is subsequently dyed. Tjaps are complicated and difficult to make, but simple metal blocks can be made by fixing metal articles to the end of wooden sticks. Copper or brass are particularly good. These can be used like a tjap by dipping the metal into wax and transferring it to the fabric. The metal should be held for a short while in the wax to heat it up, then the surplus wax should be removed by giving the stick a slight shake before printing off. After printing, the cloth is dyed, then when the cloth is dry further printing and dyeing can be carried out.

Many other materials can be used as wax

62   Wax pattern on cloth made by dipping the end of a metal block into wax and printing it off to form a resist

printing blocks such as card, wood, rope, wire, plastic, etc. All sorts of unlikely looking objects can be utilized. The only rule to apply is: if it works, use it.
Figures 62, 63

63 Wax printing block made by inserting mapping pins in the end of a cork

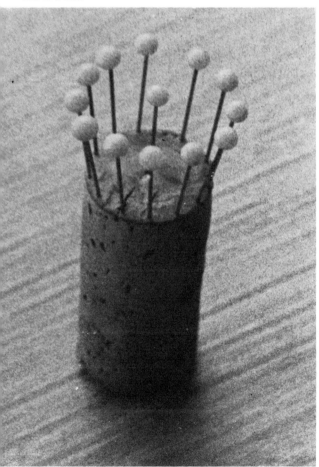

Mapping pin block

Paraffin wax, brush, heater, cold dye, spoon, gloves, bowl, newspaper, iron

Mapping pins stuck in the end of a cork make a useful little device for wax printing. The heads of the pins must all be at one level. Hold the heads of the pins in the wax so that they become well heated, then transfer the wax quickly to the surface of the cloth. To be effective the wax must sink in to the cloth.
Figures 64, 65

64 A pattern made by printing wax from mapping pins set in a cork. Each separate motif was dabbed with a brush loaded with cold dye.

65 This design was made by dipping the edge of a card into wax and pressing it onto the cloth. Wax was also splashed from a brush before dyeing

66   Wax was applied to the fabric with the pointed end of a stick and then a cold dye was painted over it

Applying wax with a stick

Paraffin wax, pointed stick, heater, cold dye, large bowl, boiler, rubber gloves, newspaper, clean rag, iron

Apply the wax to the fabric with the tip of a pointed stick or the pointed end of a paint-brush handle. As with a brush, the stick must be dipped into the wax and conveyed quickly to the cloth. A blob of wax is dropped onto the fabric and then shaped before it solidifies by dragging the stick away, to form a tail. When the wax is hard, immerse the fabric in cold dye, or paint parts of the design with dye.

Figure 66

59

Dyeing with wax barriers

Parrafin wax, brush, heater, cold dye, spoon, large bowl, boiler, rubber gloves, newspaper clean rag, iron

Interesting effects can be obtained by painting liquid dyes with a brush direct onto the fabric. They will spread by capillary action in the cloth. The wax can be used to confine the dyes within certain areas of the cloth. Breaks in the lines of the wax will allow the dye to escape, causing it to fan out. A wax pattern can be made of lines enclosing small areas of cloth, then dyes of different colours and shades painted into these areas. The lines of wax will act as barriers stopping one colour from spreading into another.

Figure 67

67 Dye painted onto the fabric and confined between lines of wax

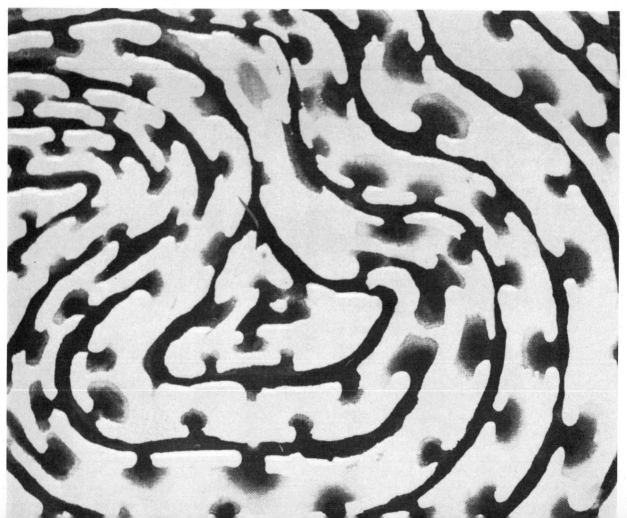

Wax rubbing

Candles or white wax crayons, heater, dye, sponge roller or brushes, spoon, boiler, rubber gloves, iron, wooden frame, drawing pins

Batik designs can be made by stretching fabric over various textured surfaces such as brickwork, gratings, wire netting, corrugated card or glass, wood grain, manhole covers and brass rubbings. The fabric is stretched across a wooden frame as tightly as possible and then put into close contact with the surface to be rubbed. If this is flat on the ground, weights can be put on the corners of the frame to prevent it moving. A stiff brush and cloth should be used on any surfaces which may need cleaning

before putting down the cloth. Plenty of newspaper should be spread over the areas which are not being rubbed, to keep the cloth clean.

Rub the candle or wax crayon firmly over the surface of the fabric. The material cannot be immersed in the dye because the colour will penetrate the back of the cloth and make the resist ineffectual. Paint or roll a thickened or pigment dye over the waxed areas and fix the dye according to the manufacturer's instructions. The wax is removed from the cloth by ironing between sheets of newspaper. In the case of pigment dyes, this will also ensure fixation.

Figure 68

68   Pattern made by wax rubbing cloth stretched over a rough wood plank

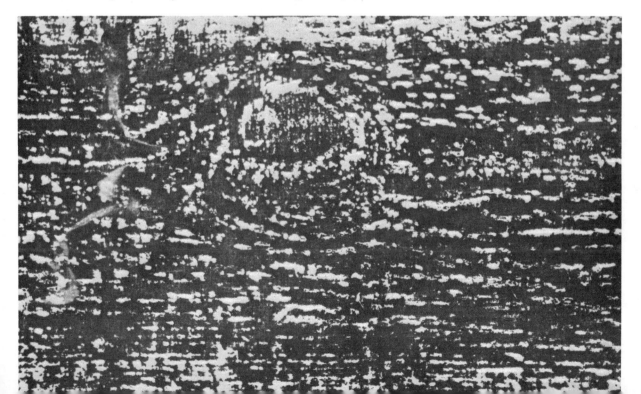

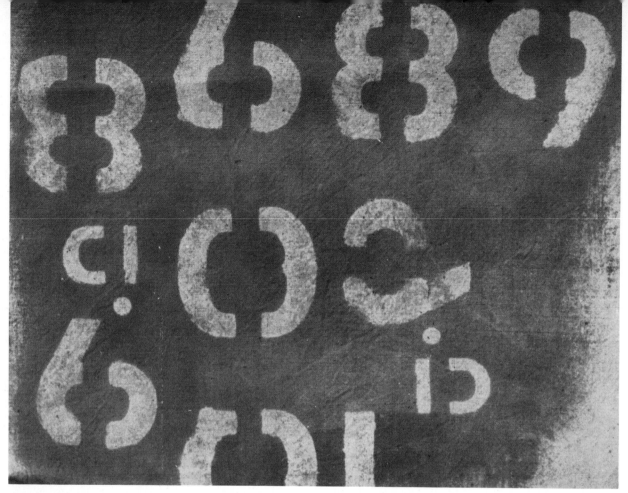

69 Detail of a flour resist stencil pattern on cloth

Flour resist

Flour, basin, fork, pottery slip trailer, icing tube or plastic container with a spout, pigment dyes, spoon, brush or sponge roller, newspaper, clean rag, iron

Flour paste can be applied to the fabric in many ways, eg with a brush or roller, to form a pattern. It can be spread over the cloth, and then a pattern combed or scratched into it while it is still wet. Stencils can be made by cutting designs in cartridge or stencil paper and the flour applied through these with a stiff brush.

When the flour is dry, a thickened pigment dye is brushed over or applied with a house decorator's roller. When the dye is completely dry, remove as much flour as possible by

62

picking or scraping it from the surface of the cloth, and then the back of the cloth is ironed. This will fix the dye. Finally wash out the cloth to remove the remainder of the flour and loose dye.
Figure 69

Cracked flour resist
Materials as above

Cracked flour resist has a distinctive veined pattern quite different from that made by wax resist. The flour paste, which should have the consistency of thick cream, is painted over the entire cloth, and when it is completely dry is squeezed in the hands so that it cracks. The fabric cannot be immersed in dye because the liquid would soften the flour and spoil the effect. Instead the dye is applied as a thick pigment with a stiff bristle brush. The colour must be forced into the cracks, and when it is dry ironed with a hot iron to fix it. The flour is then removed by squeezing the cloth and shaking off the pieces, and by scraping it carefully with a knife blade. Finally, rinse the fabric in warm water until it is clear of all flour and surplus dye.
Figure 70

70   Cracked flour resist

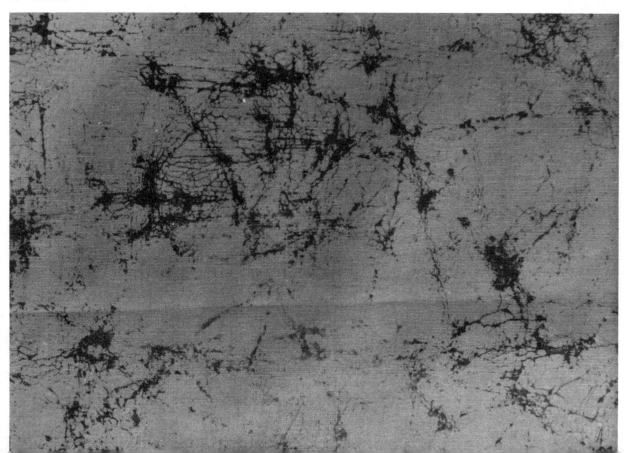

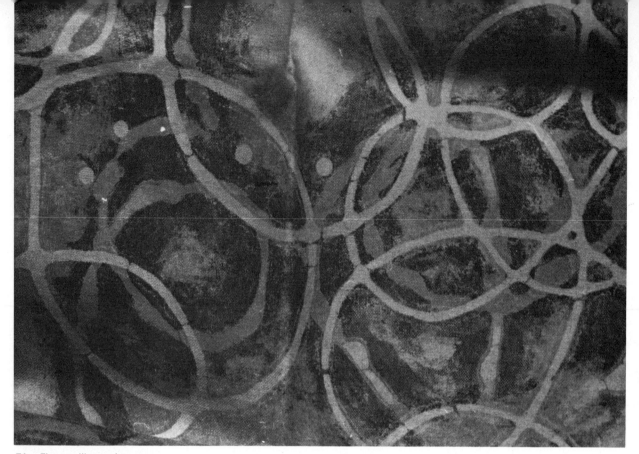

71 Flour trailing resist

Flour trailing resist

Pottery slip trailer, icing tube or plastic container with a spout, other materials as above

Mix the flour and water to the consistency of a thin cream. Pour this into the slip trailer. The flour must be free from lumps, otherwise it will not flow freely. Alternatively the flour can be put into an icing tube as used for decorating cakes, or into a plastic PVA or detergent bottle, which has a spout. Gently squeeze the container, allowing the flour to flow out smoothly to form the design. Leave the fabric spread out flat until the flour is dry, then paint pigment dye over it with a stiff brush or sponge roller. When this is dry more flour may be added over the coloured areas. Repeat the process by allowing the flour to dry and then brushing on a dye of a different colour. To remove the flour from the cloth and to fix the dye, carry out the instructions as described in the previous section.

Figure 71

Colour plate 4 Dragon Batik. *Procion* dyes on white cotton

Tie and Dye

Tie and dye is a method in which a resist is formed in the cloth by tying, stitching, or pinning, so that on immersion in dye parts of the cloth are protected from it, thus producing a pattern. When dry, more string, etc may be added to the fabric and it is then dyed again. The original bindings may be removed wholly or partly before re-tying the cloth in a different way and dying a second colour. A third or fourth colour may be added. It is usual, though not essential, to start with the lightest colour and add progressively darker shades. Binding and tying must be done very tightly to prevent dye penetration. As the action of binding can be hard on the hands, it may be necessary to wear gloves, or if these are too clumsy, bind the fingers at the vulnerable spots with adhesive tape.

This craft requires little equipment and takes up the minimum space. Basic requirements are a sink with a supply of hot and cold water, large pails or bowls to hold the dyes, a stick for stirring the dye, spoons and lots of newspapers to cover the floors and tables, plenty of clean rag for wiping up. Wooden tongs are useful for lifting the fabric from the dye, also rubber gloves to protect hands and clothing.

Darning needles and a variety of strings and thread will also be used. The scissors should be small with narrow blades, such as nail scissors. Jars with airtight lids will be required for storing dyes, etc.

To prepare the required quantity of dye, put the bound cloth in clear water so that it covers the article comfortably. Measure the water so that the amount required is known, and the dye can be prepared accordingly. Follow the manufacturer's instructions when making up the dyes. Wetting the cloth before putting it into the dye gives a sharper resist. Soft water is best for dyeing. If the water is hard, add a small amount of *Calgon*. It is a good idea to make many colour tests with various dyes on small pieces of cloth before embarking on the main work. Each piece of cloth should be numbered and a note kept of the dye formula and the length of immersion time. It is usual to dye several pieces of material in one dyebath, but remember that the dye will become progressively exhausted, and articles entered last will be paler. After dyeing, rinse the cloth both before and after unbinding till the water is clear.

Tie and die marbling

String, elastic bands, scissors, large bowl, rubber gloves, overall, stirring stick, large tongs, dye, spoons, measure, newspaper, clean rag

Squeeze the cloth into a ball shape. Tie the string tightly around the ball of cloth and wind it around in all directions. Tie off, and leave a fairly long piece of string for dipping the cloth into the dye. Prepare the dye according to the instructions. Lower the cloth into the dye-bath, but leave the string hanging over the side. Raise the cloth from time to time to judge the depth of colour. Remember the dye will always look much darker when wet. Remove

72 Marbling. A ball of cloth prepared for the dye

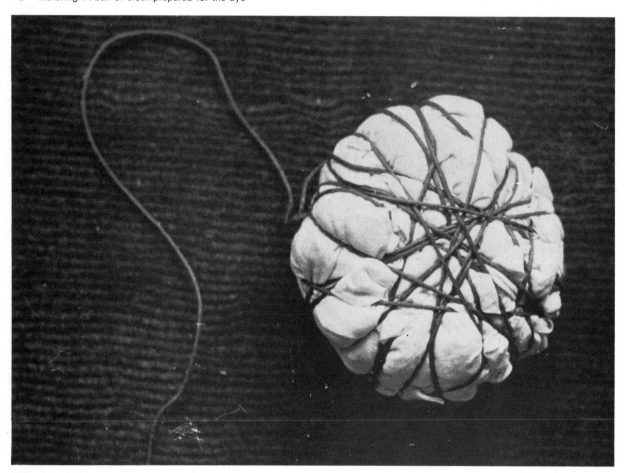

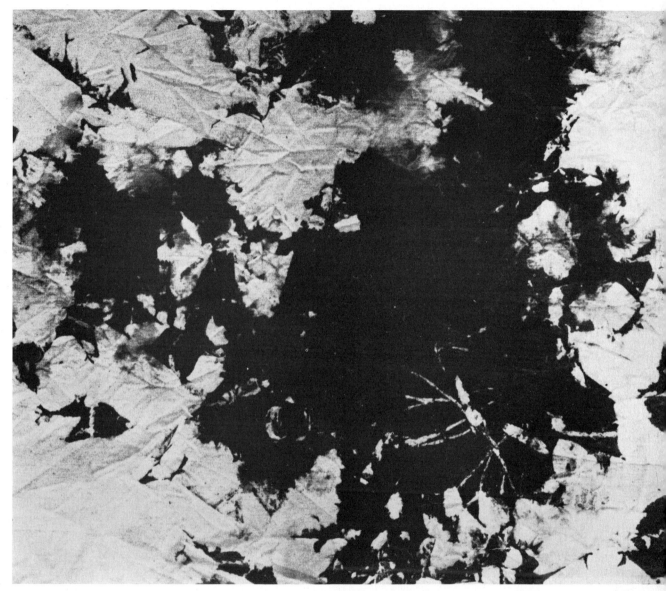

73 Marbling. After untying the ball of cloth the fabric will be only partially dyed. Re-tie with the undyed parts to the outside and dye again

the cloth from the dye and rinse in clean running water until it is clear. Undo the strings and re-arrange the cloth so that the undyed parts are towards the outside, then tie up and re-dye in the same or another colour. Repeat the process until all areas of the cloth are patterned.

Here are some other ways of marbling:

The material can be squeezed into a plastic bag. Twist elastic bands around to hold it together, then prick through the bag on all sides to let the dye in.

Push the cloth into a nylon stocking and twist elastic bands around it and then im-merse in the dye.

Put the fabric inside any porous material such as organdie, a nylon shopping bag, net or voile, or nylon marcusette, bind with string or twist elastic bands around it, and then dye.

Push the material into a plastic hair curler. Put an elastic band around the open ends to hold the cloth in, or push match-sticks across the ends for the same purpose. This is effective for small pieces of fabric.

Figures 72—74

74   The cloth can be marbled by pushing it inside a plastic hair curler and then immersing it in dye

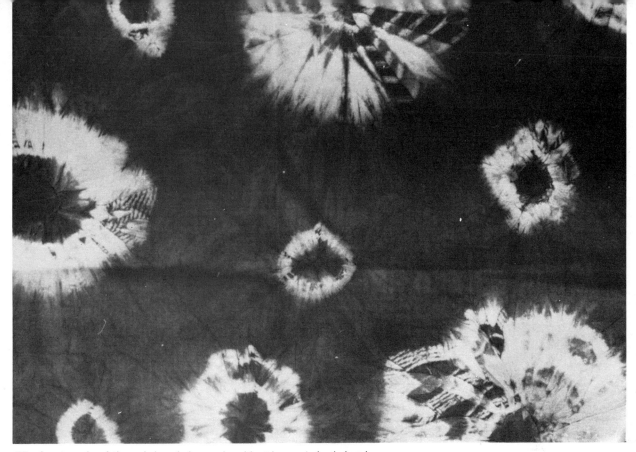

75   An example of tie and dye circles made with string and elastic bands

Tie and dye circles

String or elastic bands, large bowl, dye, spoon, stick for stirring dye, large tongs, rubber gloves, overall, scissors, clean rag, newspaper, iron

Mark the cloth with a small dot wherever a circle is required. Push the finger from behind the dot and, with the other hand, pull the cloth into a long point. Tie the string or thread around the point and bind closely and tightly along the cloth. The size of the circle will depend on the length of the binding. Continue by binding back to the beginning, then tie off. If a number of circles are required within one another, leave a space between areas of binding. String, elastic bands, raffia, pipe-cleaners, tape, are some of the other materials which can be used to bind the cloth. Each of these will give a different appearance to the design.
Figures 75, 76

69

76 Various ways of binding the cloth for tie-dyeing

Bleached tie and dye

String, elastic bands, large bowl, dye, bleach, spoon, stick for stirring, large tongs, scissors, overall, rubber gloves, iron, clean rag, newspaper

This method will give a design in reverse to conventional tie-dyeing, the cloth being dyed before binding. Ready dyed cloth can be used, but tests must be made to see that the fabric can be bleached. Many modern dyes are partially or fully bleach resistant. It is more satisfactory to dye the cloth oneself, as this means that the designer can choose the exact colour required. Also the dyes manufactured for home use are more easily bleached. When the cloth has been dyed and is dry, tie the fabric in any way desired and put it in the liquid bleach which must be made up according to the manufacturer's instructions. The tied parts of the cloth being protected from the bleach will remain, and the background colour will be bleached away. Then rinse, remove the string, rinse and iron. Of course the cloth can now be tie-dyed in the conventional way.

Figure 77

77   This piece of fabric was dyed before binding and was bleached to produce the design in reverse

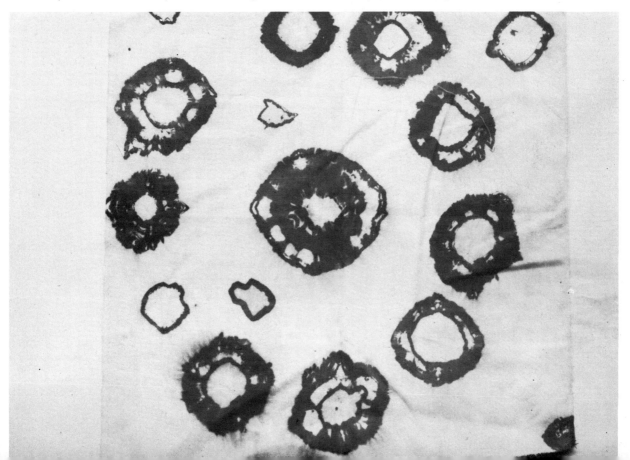

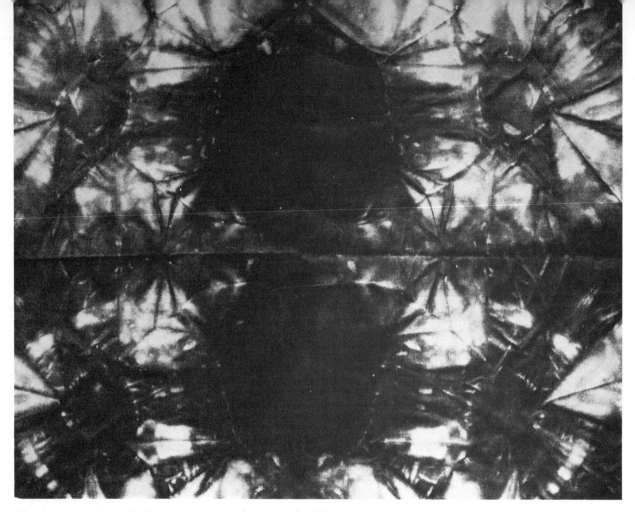

78   A design made by binding a plastic cup in the centre of a folded cloth

Objects bound in cloth

String or elastic bands, large bowl, dye, bleach, spoon, stick for stirring dye, large tongs, scissors, rubber gloves, overall, clean rag, newspaper, iron

Objects can be bound into the fabric, which may first be folded. Fruitstones, buttons, beads, marbles, bottletops, corks, shells, dried beans, stones, cotton reels, matchsticks will make different patterns depending on their size, shape and arrangement within the cloth. Mark with a pencil where each object is to go and work from the middle of the cloth outwards.

Figure 78

Tie dyeing squares of folded cloth

String, large bowl, dye, spoon, stick for stirring dye, large tongs, scissors, overall, rubber gloves, iron, clean rag, newspaper

It is a good idea to cut out and fold squares of paper to work out ideas before starting on the fabric. The cloth must be square but can be of a variety of materials. Particularly if the cloth is thick, the inside for the first dyeing may need to be brought to the outside, rebound and dyed again to complete the design.

The dotted lines in figure 79 indicate the binding and pattern, the letter 'c' indicates the centre of the cloth, and 'f' a fold.

Here are some ways of folding and tying the fabric: see figures 79 and 80.

1 Design resulting from horizontal binding below the centre

2 Where the binding is vertical below the centre the result will be like this

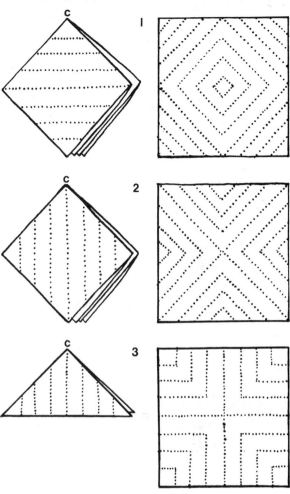

79

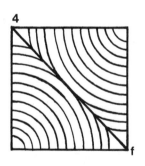

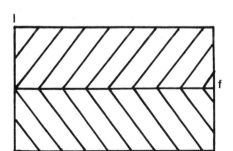

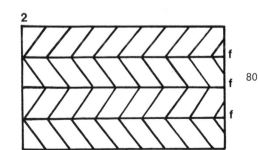

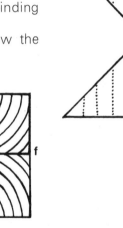

80

73

3 Fold the square into quarters diagonally, then bind vertically below the centre

4 Fold the square of fabric once diagonally. Put a pin through the two open corners into a thick carpet so that it holds firmly. Roll or pleat the cloth from the other two corners inward while pulling down away from the pin. Then tie the fabric at intervals along its length

5 Fold the cloth double. Pin the cloth in the middle of the open edges into a thick carpet. Roll or pleat the cloth from the outside inward while pulling down and away from the pin. Bind along the fabric and then dye it.
Figure 79

1 Fold the cloth double lengthways. Roll it diagonally from corner to corner, then bind at intervals along the cloth.

2 Fold the cloth double, then double it again and bind as for No 1.
Figure 80

81 Part of a square of folded cloth as in figure 72 (2)

82 *(opposite)* Part of a Chevron pattern

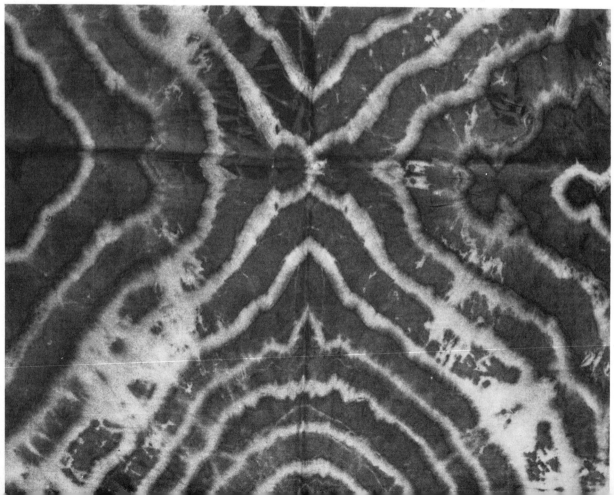

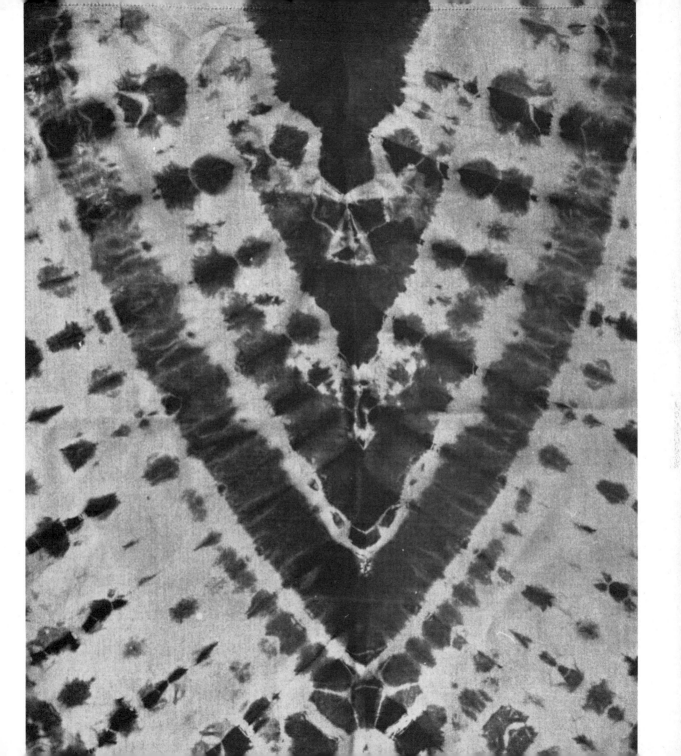

Pegs and clips

Clothes pegs or paper clips, dye, large bowl, spoon, large tongs, stick for stirring the dye, rubber gloves, clean rag, newspaper, iron

Fold the cloth into a good thickness of material. This can, of course, be done in many different ways. Then clip clothes pegs or paper clips over the folds and edges. Bulldog clips are particularly good because they are large and strong, but metal clips should not be left too long on the fabric or they will rust and mark the material. Plastic pegs will be distorted by very hot water. Each sort of clip will produce a different pattern, and the design will also depend on whether they have been put fully onto the cloth or only at the extreme edges.

Figures 83, 84

83   Folded cloth with plastic clothes clips

84   Pattern formed by putting bulldog paper clips onto a folded cloth, then dyeing it

85   Cloth sandwiched between the top and bottom of a date box before dyeing

Squeezing the cloth between sticks

String or elastic bands, sticks, large bowl, dye, spoon, large tongs, scissors, rubber gloves, overall, iron, newspaper, clean rag

Take two wooden sticks of equal size such as the bottom and top of a date box, or pieces of plywood, or ice cream sticks. Fold the cloth until it is of the same size as the sticks and sandwich it between them. Bind around the outside of the sticks with string or thick elastic bands. Dye as usual. Unfold, then refold the material with the undyed areas to the outside, then dye again.

Figure 85

Safety pin method

Safety pin, thread, dye, large bowl, scissors, large tongs, rubber gloves, overall, iron, newspaper, clean rag

Draw an outline of the shape required in pencil on the cloth. Weave a safety pin in and out all the way along this line. Bind the cloth immediately below the safety pin with thread. For symmetrical shapes, fold the cloth double and draw half the shape only against the fold, and then pin along this line. Finally the fan-shaped cloth above the pin may be bound with thread to prevent the inside of the shape being dyed.

Figures 86, 87

86   This shows how the fabric is pinned and bound for a safety pin design

87   Safety pin designs painted over with dye

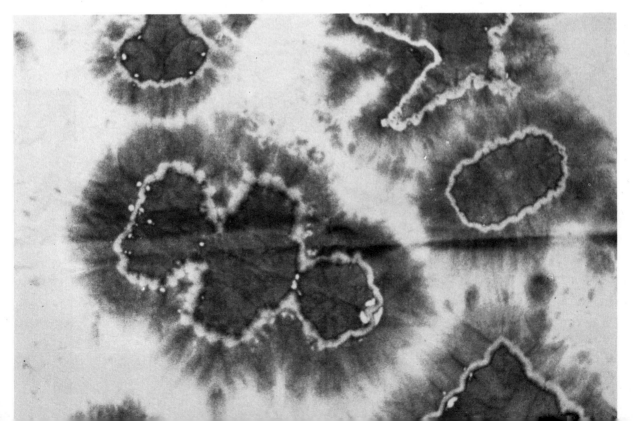

Oversewing

Needle and thread, scissors, dye, bowl, spoon, stick for stirring the dye, large tongs, rubber gloves, overall, iron, newspaper, clean rag

This method will make a band of pattern. Draw a light pencil line on the fabric of the shape of the band required. Thread a needle with strong double thread and make a large knot at the end. Fold the cloth along the pencil line and oversew this fold. The width of the band will depend on the distance the needle enters the cloth below the fold, on the thickness of fabric and thread, and on the size of the stitches. Keep the stitches moving forward. After sewing a few inches pull the cloth up very tight so that it bunches up on the thread and completely covers it. Continue sewing and when complete fasten off the thread firmly and dye.

Tie and dye with coloured string

String or thread, scissors, dye, bowl, spoon, stick for stirring the dye, large tongs, rubber gloves, overall, iron, newspaper, clean rag

If coloured string is used to bind the fabric, it may be found that the colour has partially transferred itself to the cloth. Colourless string can be dyed to produce this effect. The string is dyed in the same way as fabric, but it is not necessary to fix the dye. Just hang it up to dry before using it.

Miscellaneous Ideas

Painting on cloth
Dye, brush, gum thickening, clean rag, newspaper

Dyes can be painted, dripped or splashed with a brush onto fabric. The colour will spread by capillary action, and this can be an attractive element in the design. However, if this is not desired, mix a proportion of gum thickening with the dye before applying it to the cloth. A formula for gum thickening will be found at the end of this book. Ready prepared thickening for painting on cloth called *Paintex* is now manufactured by *Dylon*. This thickening can be washed out of the fabric after the design has been completed.

By wetting the fabric before putting on the dye, the colours can be made to spread even more in a most interesting way.
Figure 88

88   This fabric was painted with dye while wet

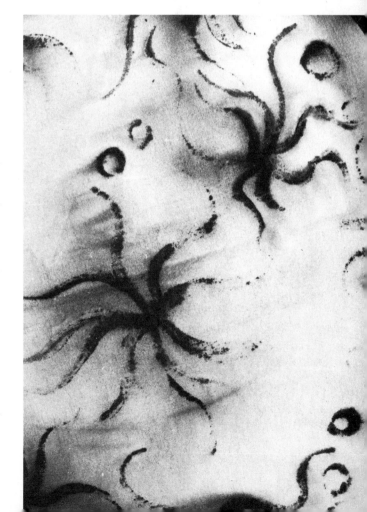

Colour plate 5 [top]   Potato print on a veined Batik background. *Helizarin* and *Procion* dyes

Colour plate 6   Potato print on a ready printed fabric

Dipping the cloth in dye

Dye, large bowl, rubber gloves, overall, newspaper, clean rag, iron

Capillary action will draw the colour into the cloth when it is dipped into the dye. If the cloth is folded, corners and edges can be dipped and symmetrical shapes easily formed.

The colour can if necessary be prevented from spreading too much by mixing a small amount of gum thickening with the dye, or the fabric can be lightly starched before dyeing. A formula for gum thickening is given at the end of this book.

Figure 89

89　Cloth folded, then dipped at the corners and edges and also painted with dye

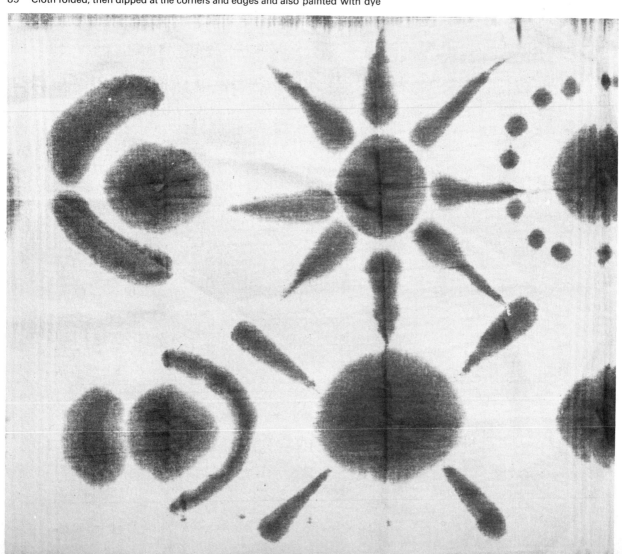

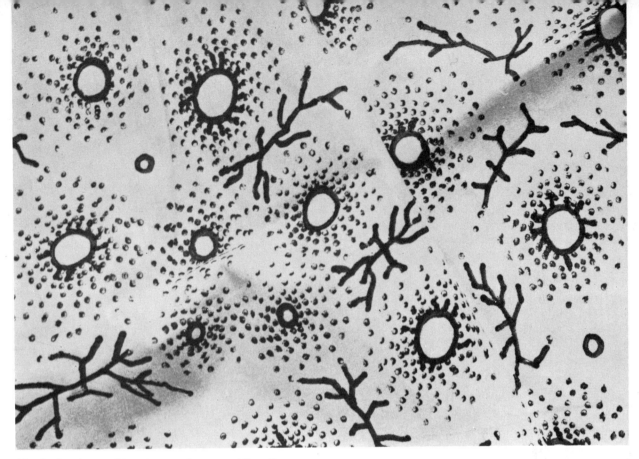

90   Design drawn with a waterproof pen on white cotton

Direct drawing on fabric

Waterproof pen, Trichem *markers,* Fineart Fabric Crayons, *natural and synthetic fabrics, cartridge paper, iron*

Some felt, fibre tip and ballpoint pens, contain waterproof inks which can be used direct onto fabric. One of these is called *Trichem,* which is a tube of ink with a ballpoint. It dries quickly and when dry it is waterproof. There are also wax crayons manufactured by the Cosmic Crayon Company for working on synthetic fabrics, called *Fineart Fabric Crayons.* These have a dye mixed with wax. They can be used direct on the cloth, or the design may first be drawn on paper. It is then put face downwards, and the back of the paper ironed. The heat setting should be appropriate to the particular cloth. The design will then be transferred in reverse onto the fabric. Ironing not only transfers the design but fixes the dye into the material.

Figure 90

91   Drawing with a tjanting filled with liquid dye on white cotton

Line patterns with a tjanting

Tjanting, liquid dye, gum thickening, newspaper, clean rag, iron

The tjanting is normally used for applying wax to the cloth for batik designs (see page 55) but it can be used to decorate the fabric with dye. The design may be lightly drawn with a pencil on the cloth before the tjanting is used. Liquid dye alone is too fluid a medium and will flow out of the tjanting too quickly. It is necessary to add a small amount of gum thickening to the dye to control the rate of flow. The quantity of thickening may have to be adjusted until the right flow is achieved. It must be free from any lumps, as these will easily block the fine tube of the tjanting.

Figure 91

Stencilling

Stencil brush, cartridge paper or stencil paper, craft knife, cutting board, dye, printing pad

Stencils can be made by using any fairly thick paper such as cartridge paper. Cut a design out of the middle of the sheet so that there is a large area of paper surrounding the stencil. The knife must be sharp to obtain a clean edge to the design. A board, such as an old drawing board or thick piece of card, is put beneath the stencil when cutting so that the table is not damaged. Retain the pieces removed when cutting. It will then be possible to use both the positive and negative shapes of the stencil. The printing pad is charged with a fairly thick dye as for block printing. Push the bristles of the stencil brush into the dye pad and, while holding the paper stencil on the cloth with the tips of the fingers, tap the colour vertically through the stencil.

Dye can also be sprayed through the stencil by putting it onto a stiff brush such as an old toothbrush, and scraping it with a knife blade. It can also be sprayed on with a fixative mouth

92 Stencil cut from cartridge paper. Stencil, brush, knife, and pad charged with dye

spray or an airbrush. In this case the dye must be very thin so that it will not block the nozzle of the spray. When spraying, the stencil should be attached to the cloth with small pieces of tape, and all the areas of fabric which are not being sprayed should be covered with newspaper to protect them. When stencilling, the colour and density of the dyes can be altered to give great variety to the design. *Figures 92, 93*

93　Stencil design using pigment dyes on white cotton material

Printing on ready printed fabric
Any materials previously mentioned

Ready printed fabrics can be used as a base for any of the methods mentioned in this book. Materials left over from dressmaking or other forms of fabric design can be put to good use in this way, and textiles of undistinguished design can be improved upon by printing over them.
Figure 94

94   Potato print over a ready printed fabric. Part of the original design has been left unprinted

Bleach designs

Bleach, dye, spoon, large tongs, rubber gloves, newspaper, clean rag, gum thickening, brush, block or screen and other printing materials, iron

Ready dyed fabrics can be used, but they may be partly or totally resistant to the bleach. It is best to dye one's own fabric. This is more interesting, and a greater control can be exercised over the finished product. Mix up a small amount of bleach according to the manufacturer's instructions. This can be used in many different ways by painting, dipping, splashing, or even drawing with a pen dipped in bleach. The dye will be removed as the bleach dries. If the dye is made up of a combination of colours, it may be possible to bleach one and leave the other. For example a purple made up of a combination of blue and red might be bleached to remove the blue and leave the red, so that the final result is a pink on a purple background.

Liquid bleach will spread in the fabric, and this can be an attractive element in the design. If this is not desired the bleach must be mixed with a gum thickening. Also for printing, when a bleach is used, it is necessary to mix a gum thickening with the dye until the necessary consistency is obtained. It can then be used for block or screen printing. Care must be taken to see that the bleach does not get on the fingers and other equipment and mark off accidentally onto the cloth. Bleach printing, which is known in the textile printing industry as 'discharge', is most useful for printing a light motif on a dark background where there is the problem of joining a repeat design.
Figure 95

95   Bleach design painted with a fine brush on pre-dyed fabric

96 An example of flock printing. Half the design has been flocked and the other half has been left unflocked, showing the adhesive

Flock printing

Flock and flock adhesive

This technique gives a slightly raised pattern of coloured wool or rayon powder on the fabric. A strong waterproof adhesive is applied to the cloth by painting or printing. For block printing the adhesive must be capable of adhering to the block, and in the case of screen printing of passing easily through the screen. PVA or an oil-based printing ink can be used.

This should be the same colour as the flock. Flock and adhesive are manufactured for this purpose, and information is given on these at the end of the book. While the adhesive is still wet on the fabric, sprinkle the flock powder over it, then shake the surplus off into a receptacle so that it can be re-used. Allow the adhesive to dry thoroughly.
Figure 96

89

Can print

Tin can, pigment dye

Cut the top and bottom from a tin can. The width of the stripe to be printed will depend upon the diameter of the can used. Mark out the fabric with threads or with lightly pencilled lines. Put the can on one end of the fabric, and half fill it with dye pigment which should be of the consistency of thick cream.

Slide the can along the lines keeping it firmly pressed against the cloth all the time. As there will be a tendency for rings to form when the tin is stopped, an uninterrupted run is required. An area of fabric will be needed to reverse the direction of the tin at either end of the material. When dry, iron the fabric on the reverse side.

Figure 97

97 A can print

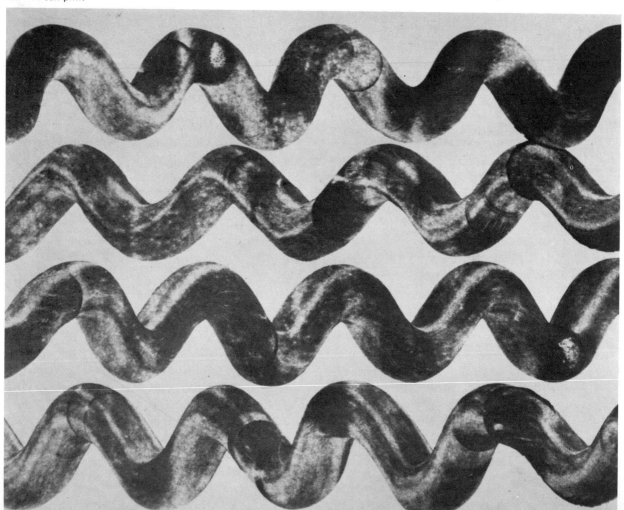

98　Large communal work. A screen printed fabric designed and executed by several teenage pupils

Communal fabric designs

Working with a large group of people, as in a classroom, affords an opportunity for large scale fabric designs which may be used, for example, for wall hangings, room dividers, curtains, or bedcovers. They may be made by screen or block printing, tie dyeing or batik, or dye painting, or a mixture of the methods previously described in this book. Apart from other considerations, the number of persons able to work together will be limited by the size of the material, in which case the class may be divided into work groups, each with their own large separate piece of fabric. A communal fabric design made by one of the printing methods previously mentioned may be composed from many individual blocks or screenprints. However, the material can be divided up into individual pieces, and when each person has completed his or her piece these can be assembled by sewing or sticking them together to make one large work. This is particularly suitable for batik or tie dyeing. The communal design may be a collage or appliqué made from remnants of previous dressmaking or fabric printing work, and these can be attached to a background of heavier material, such as canvas or a hardboard panel. *Figure 98*

Potential uses for fabric designs

There is a natural link between fabric printing and needlework. Great pleasure and benefit can be derived by carrying out the creative process from plain fabric to the final made up article. When fabric is printed for a particular purpose, thought must be given to the suitability of the pattern to the material, its purpose, and the surroundings in which it will be used. For example, curtain material will tend to have larger motifs than that used on a dress fabric. Colours and designs suitable for a bedroom would not necessarily be appropriate to a kitchen.

Among the many articles which can be made up from the printed material are: shirts, blouses, skirts, shorts, jeans, dresses, aprons, ties, swimsuits, beach bags, scarves, head-scarves, belts, curtains, coverlets, tablemats, tablecloths, napkins, dolls' and puppets' clothes, costumes for plays, soft toys, cushions, handkerchiefs, towels, pillowcases, room dividers, wall hangings, chair covers.
Figure 99

99 Soft toy made from tie and dye fabric

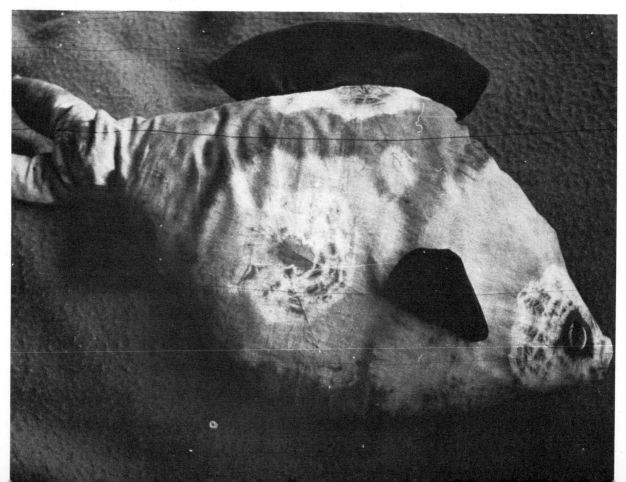

Fabric design, embroidery and appliqué

Any materials for fabric design. Sewing machine or needle, thread, wool, and a variety of beads, buttons, sequins and fabrics

The design can first be made on the fabric using any of the methods previously described. For example, a simple design can be made by printing from a leaf as described on page 14. When this is dry, work over it with embroidery stitches. Experiment with different textures and colours in wool, stranded cotton, coton-à-broder, *Sylko Perle*, and other types of thread. Use a variety of stitches such as straight, chain, fly, cretan, herringbone, spider. Couching adds interest to a simple design, and the work can be enhanced with beads, sequins, buttons, metallic thread, feathers, and any other interesting articles that will lend themselves to the printed pattern.

The design can also be made by cutting out paper shapes. Tracings are made of these, and then cut out in thin card. These are lightly padded and covered with different textures of fabric. All the raw edges must be tacked securely on the wrong side. These shapes can be glued to the printed background material and stitched from the wrong side with large tacking stitches.

Formulae

For simplicity and because these are the ones which are most familiar to the author, only a few recipes are given below. There are many others, some of which will be found in the books listed in the bibliography or can be provided by the manufacturers.

Helizarin TS125 Pigment Dye for application by screen, brush, spray, etc.
Helizarin colour, one to two teaspoons.
Helizarin binder, one pint.
When dry, iron the back of the fabric for five minutes at 140°C.

Dylon Cold Dyes for tie dyeing and batik (see manufacturer's instructions).

Procion M Cold Water Dyes for batik only. Colour penetration is too great for tie and dye. Mix five tablespoons of salt in a 1 kg (2 lb) jar of hot water. Mix two tablespoons of soda in another 1 Kg (2 lb) jar of hot water.
Mix a small amount of dye with cold water in a separate container, then fill up with warm water until the dye is transparent. Fill a large plastic bowl half full with cold water and add the dye; add the salt and soda just before putting in the cloth.
After adding salt and soda the dye will only last about three hours. To fix the dye leave the fabric exposed at room temperature overnight.

Manutex Gum Thickening for mixing with dyes to make printing and discharge pastes.
One dessert-spoonful of *Calgon* to a 1 Kg (2 lb) jar of cold water.
Add one teaspoonful of *Manutex*. Stir for 2 minutes. Leave for 2 hours.

Dygon Super Paintex gum thickening can be used for mixing with *Dylon* dyes (see manufacturer's instructions).

Gum Arabic can be used as a thickening, and to fasten the cloth to the printing table.
Soak the powder in cold water. Boil for two to three hours, cool and strain.

Household Bleach can be used for bleaching fabrics and for application by brush, etc.
Dilute one part of bleach with three parts water. A stronger solution may rot the fabric.

Dygon can be used for bleaching fabrics and application with a brush, etc.
For block and screen printing these need to be mixed with gum thickening.

Formosol Discharge Printing Paste is another alternative.
Mix three parts of *Formosol*,
one part glycerine,
four parts of water,
twelve parts of gum thickening.
After printing iron with a damp cloth or steam iron.

Bibliography

General books on fabric printing

Fabric Printing, Gisella Hein, Batsford London, Van Nostrand Reinhold New York
Creative Textile Craft: Thread and Fabric, Rolf Hartung, Batsford London, Van Nostrand Reinhold New York
Colour and Texture in Creative Textile Craft, Rolf Hartung, Batsford London, Van Nostrand Reinhold New York
Introducing Textile Printing, Nora Proud, Batsford London, Watson-Guptill New York

An Introduction to Textile Printing, W Clark, Butterworths London
Fabric Printing by Hand, Steven Russ, Studio Vista London
Print your own Fabrics, Jutta Lamner, Batsford London, Watson-Guptill New York
Fabric Printing and Dyeing, David Green, MacGibbon and Kee London
Dyed and Printed Fabrics, June Hobson, Dryad Press Leicester
Design on Fabrics, M P Johnstone and G Kaufman, Van Nostrand Reinhold New York
Wall Hangings of Today, Vera Sherman, Mills and Boon London, Branford Massachusetts
Decorative Papers and Fabrics, A Hollander, Van Nostrand Reinhold New York
Textiles: Properties and Behaviour, Edward Miller, Batsford London

Screen Printing

Introducing Screen Printing, Anthony Kinsey, Batsford London, Watson-Guptill New York
Screen Printing on Fabric, Valerie Searle and Roberta Clayson, Studio Vista London, Watson-Guptill New York
Silk Screen Printing, Brian Elliott, Oxford University Press London and New York
Silk Screen Printing for Beginners, Gordon Terry, Heinemann London
Screen Process Printing, Will Clemence, Blandford London
Photographic Screen Process Printing, Albert Kosloff, Signs of the Times Publishing Company Cincinnati

Photography

Photography without a Camera, Patra Holter, Studio Vista London, Van Nostrand Reinhold New York
Introducing Photograms, Pierre Bruandet, Batsford London, Watson-Guptill New York
Making Photograms, Virna Haffer, Focal Press London and New York
Photography for Designers, Julian Sheppard, Focal Press London and New York

Block Printing

Creative Print Making, Peter Green, Batsford London, Watson-Guptill New York
Introducing Surface Printing, Peter Green, Batsford London, Watson-Guptill New York
Lino Cuts and Wood Cuts, Michael Rothenstein, Studio Vista London
Simple Print Making, C Kent and M Cooper, Studio Vista London

Batik

Introducing Batik, Evelyn Samuel, Batsford London, Watson-Guptill New York
Batik, Nik Krevitsky, Van Nostrand Reinhold New York
Designing in Batik and Tie Dye, Nancy Belfer, Davis Publications New York
Getting Started in Batik, Astrith Deyrup, Collier Macmillan London, Bruce Publishing Company New York

Tie and Dye

Tie and Dye made Easy, Anne Maile, Mills and Boon London, Taplinger New York
Tie and Dye as a Present Day Craft, Anne Maile, Mills and Boon London, Taplinger New York
Tie Dye, Sara Néa, Van Nostrand Reinhold New York

Appliqué and Embroidery

Embroidery and Fabric Collage, Eirian Short, Pitman London
Machine Embroidery, Jennifer Gray, Batsford London, Van Nostrand Reinhold New York
Appliqué, E Shers and D Fielding, Pitman London, Watson-Guptill New York

Suppliers

General printing equipment

E J Arnold (School Suppliers), Butterley Street, Leeds LS101AX
Dryad, Northgates, Leicester
Griffin and George Ltd, PO Box 13, Wembley, Middlesex HA0 1LD
Nottingham Handcraft Company (School Suppliers), Melton Road, West Bridgford, Nottingham NG2 6HD

Fabrics

Emil Adler, 46 Mortimer Street, Lonwon W1
Bradley Textiles Company, 15 Stott Street, Nelsons, Lancashire
Joshua Hoyle and Sons Ltd, 12 Bow Lane, London EC4
John Lewis and Co Ltd, Oxford Street, London W1A 1EX
Limericks, 89 Hamlet Court Road, Westcliff-on-Sea, Essex

Tables and coverings

Macclesfield Engineering and Sheet Metal Co Ltd, Windmill Street, Macclesfield, Cheshire
Dunlop Rubber Co Ltd, 2 Cambridge Street, Manchester (*for waterproof sheeting*)

Block printing equipment

All equipment can be obtained from the firms listed under general printing equipment
Albright and Wilson Ltd, PO 28, Beckwith Knowle, Harrogate, Yorkshire (*for Formasul*)

Screen printing equipment

Sericol Group, 24 Parsons Green Lane, London SW6
E T Marler Ltd, 191 Western Road, Merton Abbey, London SW19
Pronk, Davis and Rushby Ltd, 90–96 Brewery Road, London N7
George Nelson Dale and Co Ltd, Enscote Mills, Warwick (*for photographic gelatine*)
B Young and Co Ltd, 123 Grange Road, London SE1 (*for photographic gelatine*)
A J Purdy and Co Ltd, 248 Lea Bridge Road, Leyton E10 (*for laquer*)
Vanguard Manufacturing Co Ltd, Bridge Road, Maidenhead, Berkshire (*for opaque inks, Photopake*)
Lancro Chemicals Ltd, Salters Lane, Eccles, Manchester, and 12 Whitehall, London SW1 (*for Lancro table adhesive*)

Batik equipment

All equipment can be obtained from the firms listed under general printing equipment

Alec Tiranti Ltd, 72 Charlotte Street, W1 (*for paraffin wax, beeswax and tjantings*)

D Mackay, 83 East Road, Cambridge (*for tjantings*)

Dyes

Dylon International Ltd, Worsley Bridge Road, Lower Sydenham, London SE26 (*for Procion M Dyes and Dylon Cold Dyes*)

Magros Ltd, Monument Way West, Woking, Surrey (*for Magros Fabricol Dyes*)

Skilbeck Brothers Ltd, Bagnall House, 55–57 Glengall Road, London SE15 (*for Helizarin Dyes*)

Winsor and Newton, Wealdstone, Harrow, Middlesex (*for Printex Dyes*)

Reeves and Sons Ltd, Lincoln Road, Enfield, Middlesex EN1 1SX (*for Reeves Craft Dyes*)

George Rowney and Co Ltd, 12 Percy Street, London W1A 2BP (*for Rowney Fabric Printing Dyes*)

Photographic materials

Kodak Ltd, High Holburn, London WC1 (*for Kodatrace, TP Paper and all other photographic supplies*)

General equipment

Magros Ltd, Monument Way West, Woking, Surrey (*for PVA adhesive [Marvin Medium]*)

Cosmic Crayon Co Ltd, Amptill, Bedford (*for Fineart Fabric Crayons*)

Alginate Industries Ltd, Walter House, Bedford Street, London WC2 (*for Manutex*)

Letraset Ltd, St George's House, 195–203 Waterloo Road, London SE1 (*for Letraset, Letrafilm, etc*)

Harrington Brothers Ltd, Weir Road, Balham, London SW12, (*for gum arabic*)

Spicer Cowan Ltd, 19 Newbridge Street, London EC4 (*for paper*)

Spray Technique Ltd, Moor Top Works, Moor Top Place, Heaton Moor, Stockport, Cheshire, SK4 4JB (*for flock and adhesive*)

USA

General printing equipment, etc (mail order)

American Handicrafts Co Inc, 20 West 14th Street, New York. NY 10011

Ferzandie and Sperrie Inc, 103 Lafayette Street, New York, NY 10013

Silk Screen Supplies Inc, 32 Lafayette Avenue, Brooklyn, New York, NY 11217 (*for screen printing equipment*)

Atlas Silk Screen Supply, 1733 Milwaukee Avenue, Chicago, Illinois 60647 (*for screen printing equipment*)

Rapid Roller Co Ltd, 5050 South Kedzie Avenue, Chicago, Illinois 60632 (*for rubber rollers*)

Mantrol Co, Div Millmaster Oynx Corporation, 99 Park Avenue, New York, NY 10016 (*for shellac products*)

Bradshaw-Praeger and Co, 3252 West 47th Place, Chicago, Illinois 60632 (*for shellac products*)

Stein Hall and Co Inc, 605 Third Avenue, New York, NY 10016 (*for Manutex [Halltex], British Gum [Dextrin]*)

Dyes

School Products Co Inc, 312 East 32nd Street, New York, NY 10010 (*Dylon Cold and Dylon Paintex*)

J C Larson Co Inc, 7330 North Clark Street, Chicago, Illinois 60626 (*for Dylon Cold and Dylon Paintex*)

American Cyanamid Co, Dyes Division, Wayne, New Jersey 07470 (*for Helizarin [Alizarin]*)

Winsor and Newton Inc, 555 Winsor Drive, Secaucus, New Jersey 07094 (*for Printex Fabric Printing Colours*)

Pylam Products Co Inc, 95–100 218th Street, Queen's Village, New York, NY 11429 (*for Procion*)

Peral Paint Co, 308 Canal Street, New York, NY 10013 (*distributors of Rowney Fabric Dyes*)

Regents Products, 251 East Grand Chicago, Illinois 60611 (*distributors of Rowney Fabric Dyes*)

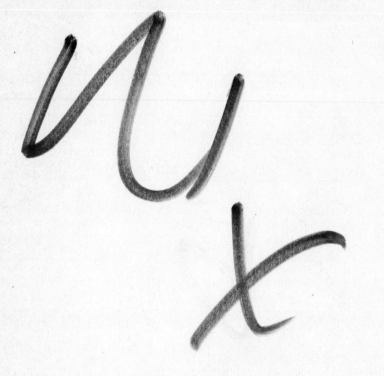